Contents

Introduction

This handbook has been written for students learning about Citizenship in secondary schools. It provides a comprehensive background with an emphasis on global issues. Aimed at students at Key Stages 3 and 4, the handbook has many possible uses including as a course book, homework aid or reference source.

It aims to help you to learn about the world around you by exploring basic concepts such as power, fairness, social justice, democracy and diversity.

Questions and activities are included at the end of each chapter. These can be used as the basis for discussion, debate or research. You can work individually or in groups, as directed by your teacher. The Web sites listed on pages 115 to 117 are intended to act as starting points for research work. A glossary is provided on pages 118 to 124.

Using this book

If this is your own book, you may decide to personalise it. For example, fill in the spaces on page ii, make notes in the margin, add to the list of Web sites or add to the glossary.

Feedback

If you have any comments or suggestions as to how this book may be improved, please send them to the authors via Pearson Publishing.

Name ....

Class ....

School ....

....

....

....

Further copies of this publication may be obtained from:

Pearson Publishing
Chesterton Mill, French's Road, Cambridge CB4 3NP
Tel 01223 350555   Fax 01223 356484

Email info@pearson.co.uk   Web site www.pearsonpublishing.co.uk

ISBN 1 85749 719 8

Published by Pearson Publishing 2002
© Pearson Publishing 2002

1 Human rights

First they [the Nazis] came for the Communists, but I was not a Communist so I did not speak out. Then they came for the Socialists and the Trade Unionists, but I was neither, so I did not speak out. Then they came for the Jews, but I was not a Jew so I did not speak out. And when they came for me, there was no one left to speak out for me.

Martin Niemoeller, Pastor,
German Evangelical (Lutheran) Church

What are human rights?

Human rights are about the **respect for each individual human life and for human dignity**. Ideas about human rights can be found in different philosophies and religions throughout history. However, in the last 50 years, after the horrors of the Second World War, greater international attention has been given to human rights.

If we're defending human dignity, why am I wearing this costume?

Human rights can protect us from the actions of others that could threaten our freedom or dignity. The idea behind human rights is that we all have human rights simply because we are human. It does not matter what race, colour, sex or religion we are or how wealthy we are, human rights mean that we are entitled to the same rights as every other person. We say that these rights are **inalienable** because **no person or state** has the right to take them away from us for any reason.

Why are human rights important?

Human rights are important in the relationships that exist between individuals and the government that has power over them. The government exercises power over its people. However, human rights mean that this power is limited. States have to look after the basic needs of the people and protect some of their freedoms. Some of the most important features of human rights are the following:

- They are for everyone.
- They are internationally guaranteed.
- They are protected by law.
- They focus on the dignity of the human being.
- They protect individuals and groups.
- They cannot be taken away.

Human rights declarations

Some basic human rights have been written down and agreed to by many states. The most famous text is the **Universal Declaration of Human Rights (UDHR)** which the UN General Assembly approved on 10 December 1948. International Human Rights Day is now celebrated on 10 December every year. The statement of principles in the Declaration has had a great influence all over the world, although governments are not forced by law to obey them. However, many lawyers would argue that because of the way the international world works, human rights have become legally binding and that governments now do have to obey some of the principles.

Some of the human rights and freedoms listed in the Universal Declaration of Human Rights and in other treaties (often called covenants, conventions or guidelines) include:

- The right to life.
- Freedom from discrimination.
- The right for everyone to be treated equally by the law.

- Freedom to have privacy in the family, home or with personal correspondence.
- Freedom of association, expression, assembly (gathering in groups) and movement.
- The right to seek and enjoy asylum (a safe home).
- The right to a nationality.
- Freedom of thought, conscience and religion.
- The right to vote and take part in government.
- The right to fair working conditions.
- The right to adequate food, shelter, clothing and social security.
- The right to health.
- The right to education.
- The right to property.
- The right to participate in cultural life.
- The right to development.

- Freedom from torture and cruel, inhuman or degrading treatment or punishment.
- Freedom from arbitrary arrest or detention.
- The right to a fair trial.

When the Declaration was created, most states agreed to it. However, some countries did not sign the Declaration. At the time, South Africa was dominated by white people who did not want equal rights for black people and so did not sign. Saudi Arabia also opposed the Declaration for religious reasons. One of the Articles (18) allows humans the freedom to change and practise the religion of their choice. Laws in Saudi Arabia mean that the practise of Christianity is forbidden and the right to change your religion from Islam to another is not recognised in Islamic ideology. The Government of the former Soviet Union and former communist countries, despite agreeing with much of it, also did not sign the Declaration, because they suspected that it was a Cold War (see page 110) text that threatened their authority.

History of the human rights movement

The concept of human rights has existed in European thought for many centuries, even at the time of King John of England (1166-1216), who signed the Magna Carta in 1215. This listed a few basic human rights including the right of the Church to be free from Government interference, the right of free citizens to own property and to be free from large taxes.

The eighteenth- and nineteenth-century European philosophers talked about 'natural rights', ie rights belonging to a person by nature and because they are human, not just because they were a citizen of a particular country or members of a religious or ethnic group.

In the eighteenth century, two important revolutions took place. In 1776, most British colonies in North America declared their independence from the British Empire in the US Declaration of Independence. The most famous words from this declaration are:

We hold these truths to be self-evident; that all men are created equal, that they are endowed by their Creator with certain unalienable rights, that among these are life, liberty and the pursuit of happiness.

Sorry, Mrs Washington, George has gone out for the night... Said something about life, liberty and the pursuit of happiness!

In 1789, the people of France overthrew their monarchy and set up the first French Republic. They, too, produced a text on the Declaration of the Rights of Man.

The middle and late nineteenth century saw human rights issues taking centre stage. These issues included slavery, brutal working conditions, starvation wages and child labour.

For the first half of the twentieth century, many civil rights and human rights movements influenced social change. Labour unions brought about laws that gave workers the right to strike, setting minimum working conditions, forbidding or improving child labour, and a 40-hour working week was set up in many European countries. The women's rights movement gained the right to vote for many women. National liberation movements in many countries succeeded in driving out colonial powers. One of the most influential was Mahatma Ghandi's peaceful movement to free India from British rule.

Amnesty International

Amnesty International is a non-governmental organisation (NGO) or pressure group that has a large membership.

In 1961, a group of lawyers, journalists and writers who were upset by the sentencing of two Portuguese college students to 20 years in prison for having raised their glasses in a toast to 'freedom', formed the Appeal for Amnesty. The appeal told the stories of six 'prisoners of conscience' from different countries jailed for peacefully expressing their political or religious beliefs, and called on governments to free them.

A simple plan of action was to call for appeals to be made on behalf of these prisoners and anyone else who, like them, had been imprisoned for peacefully expressing their beliefs.

The response to this appeal was larger than anyone expected. The appeal grew and Amnesty International and the modern human rights movement were born. The modern human rights movement demands that governments everywhere, regardless of ideology, follow certain basic principles of human rights in the treatment of their citizens.

This appeals to people, especially those who are not interested in joining a large political movement. They just want to speak out against any government that dares to abuse, imprison, torture or kill human beings whose only crime is to express beliefs that are different from their government and saying so publicly. They write letters to governments and broadcast the plights of these people in the hope of persuading or embarrassing governments to act in a better manner.

Amnesty International does not take positions on all issues which people view as human rights concerns (such as abortion) and does not promote or criticise any form of government. While it wants a fair trial for all political prisoners, it does not help '**prisoners of conscience**' who have used or supported violence. It does work, however, to abolish torture and the death penalty.

Some people find this too limited. Many pro-democracy supporters were upset when the organisation dropped Nelson Mandela (at the time, a black South African anti-apartheid activist in jail) from its list of adopted prisoners, because of his support for a violent struggle against **apartheid**.

Over the years, the number of human rights groups has increased, and recognition for such movements has grown. In 1977, Amnesty International was awarded the Nobel Peace Prize for its work.

What laws are there to protect human rights?

No one shall be subjected to torture or cruel, inhuman or degrading treatment or punishment.

UN Declaration Article 5

Human rights in South Africa

South Africa used to be dominated by white people under a system that was known as 'apartheid'. Many Western businesses flourished there. Black people living there were extremely poor, had few rights, were often imprisoned for no reason and were not given the same opportunities in education and employment as white people. They could not even vote for a government that would consider their needs. Children who were black were sent to different, poorer schools and treated as second-class citizens; many could not even go to school.

However, international public opinion and African-American pressure groups campaigned against the way in which black people were being treated until, eventually, businesses and banks did not want to be seen to trade with South Africa. This international pressure helped the decision of the South African regime to talk with the African National Congress and, eventually, apartheid was stopped.

And now the South African national anthem – first, the white notes...

What could you do if you faced this kind of treatment?

If you lived in a country governed by the rule of law, you could appeal to the courts at home to help you. However, if a European does not feel understood by the courts in their country, then the dispute can be taken to the **European Commission on Human Rights** and the **European Court of Human Rights**. In non-European countries, there is no such court of appeal, but the standards that have been set internationally have a moral influence. However, international human rights do not have as great an influence as many wish for; after all, the death penalty is still used widely in the United States, despite many campaigns against it.

Human rights law means that governments are able to do some things and are stopped from doing others. For example, the British Government would be stopped from making a law that excluded women from voting or one that stated that all Asian people could not have free education. These laws would not consider the fact that we are all human, they would discriminate against women or Asian people.

Where does human rights law come from?

Human rights law comes from two main international sources:

- **Customary international law** (or 'custom') is law that develops through time and has become a consistent practice of states. In other words, if, over a period of time, states act in a certain way because they all believe that they should, that behaviour comes to be seen as a principle of international law (even if it is not written down in an agreement). So, even though the Universal Declaration of Human Rights is not binding, certain parts of the Declaration are considered to be customary international law.

- **Treaty laws** are the laws of human rights set out in international agreements (like the UN Declaration) that are developed, agreed to and kept by countries. Some treaties focus on particular groups to be protected, such as The Convention on the Rights of the Child.

Who monitors human rights?

Clearly, just having sets of rules is not enough to ensure that they are kept. Human rights standards are monitored at several levels. There are national institutions and organisations that monitor human rights such as:

- The courts.
- Parliament.
- The media.
- Government and independent human rights commissions.
- Human rights groups and other non-governmental organisations.
- Community-based organisations.
- Professional associations (such as lawyers' or doctors' associations).
- Trade unions.
- Religious organisations.
- Academic institutions.

Some human rights treaties establish a group of experts (a 'treaty body', such as the Human Rights Committee) whose main job is to monitor how countries implement the treaty. Three bodies look at individual complaints of abuses of human rights – the Human Rights Committee, the Committee on the Elimination of Racial Discrimination and the Committee Against Torture.

What is the job of the High Commissioner for Human Rights at the UN?

The High Commissioner for Human Rights is part of the Secretariat for the UN (see *Chapter 8*). The aim of their role is to:

- promote and protect all civil, cultural, economic, political and social rights
- coordinate education and public information programmes in the field of human rights and provide advice and assistance

- talk with all governments to make sure they all respect human rights and help prevent human rights violations in the world
- carry out tasks assigned to them by the UN system in the field of human rights and promote all human rights.

How is human rights law enforced?

International human rights law means that individual countries are responsible for keeping to human rights laws. This means, for example, that states should make sure that any victims are compensated and that people who abuse human rights are punished. Thus, it is up to each state to enforce law through their own courts.

Sometimes, countries cannot or will not deal with human rights abuses and so they may have to give up or transfer an offender elsewhere. Treaties, like the Convention Against Torture and Other Cruel, Inhuman or Degrading Treatment or Punishment, mean that states may be told to send the offenders to be tried elsewhere.

In the 1990s, after the genocide and crimes against humanity in Rwanda and the former Yugoslavia, tribunals (courts) were set up by the United Nations Security Council to bring people who were responsible for human rights abuses to justice. Following this, the international community thought that it would be important to set up a permanent International Criminal Court (this is based in Rome).

What is the European Convention of Human Rights (ECHR)?

The Council of Europe is a group of nations that came together after the Second World War to stop atrocities which took place during the war from happening again. It is separate from the European Union (EU) and has its own Court of Human Rights in Strasbourg. Before, if you had a human rights complaint in Britain that was not being dealt with, you could take your case to the court in Strasbourg to claim your rights under the ECHR. Now the ECHR is part of our UK law so, if you have a complaint about your human rights, you could take a public authority to court.

What is the Human Rights Act in the UK?

On 2 October 2000, the Human Rights Act became part of UK law. The rights and freedoms in the ECHR were incorporated into our law. There are 16 basic rights in the Act that affect your rights in everyday life: what you can say, do or believe in.

These include the right to **life**; the right **not to be tortured, treated as a slave** or having to do **forced labour**; the right to a **fair trial** and the right to **respect for private and family life** and your **correspondence**. You also have the right to **freedom of thought, conscience** and **religion**. This means that you are free to hold a broad range of views, beliefs and thoughts. Next to this is the right to **freedom of expression**, which means you have the right to hold opinions and express your views, even if they are not popular (sometimes, this right may be restricted).

There is also the right to **freedom of assembly and association**, meaning that you can meet with whom you please in a peaceful way and join with people you choose. You also have the right to **marry** and **start a family**.

Importantly, you have the right to **protection of property** and a right to **education**. There is also the right to **free elections** and **the prohibition of discrimination**, which means that you have the right not to be treated differently because of your race, religion, sex, colour, political views or any other status.

Freedom of thought

What if you feel your rights have not been respected by a public authority?

The Human Rights Act does not really say what a public authority is, but it includes all government departments, local authorities, the police, prison, immigration officers, public prosecutors, courts and tribunals, non-departmental public bodies (NDPBs) or anyone that exercises a public function.

If you think that a public authority has abused your rights, you can take the authority to court. If the court finds that a public authority has breached your rights, it can award whatever seems just. This could include payment of money to compensate you, known as damages.

Questions

1 Why are human rights important?

2 Why do you think the UN Declaration on Human Rights happened in 1948?

3 Which human right is the most important to you? For example, is it the right to education or equal treatment, or the freedom to practise your religion, or is it to be protected from torture?

4 Can we force a country to respect human rights? What about Turkey, where prisoners are tortured in jails?

5 What can the rest of the world do if human rights are being abused in a certain country?

6 Do we have the right to tell other countries how to treat their citizens or should we not interfere?

Note: For some of these questions there are not necessarily any right or wrong answers. Some of these issues have been debated for years.

Activity

Research the women's rights movement. Since when have women been allowed to vote in the UK? Why do you think it was only in the twentieth century that women were given the vote?

2 The media and its role in society

What is the media?

The **media** is a collective term which usually describes those organisations or 'agencies' that provide the public with news and information. It includes radio, television, newspapers, magazines and the Internet. The media enables us to communicate, thus exchanging and sharing information and ideas. It can have a variety of purposes; for example, it can inform, persuade people to buy products, educate, influence people's ideas and entertain.

A brief history of the media

- **Eighteenth century** – Widespread circulation of newspapers in Europe and North America.
- **Nineteenth century** – Introduction of the postal service in the UK (1850s) and invention of the telephone (1876).
- **Twentieth century** – First live radio broadcast by the BBC (1922); first television broadcast by the BBC (1927); World Wide Web and electronic mail made available to the public (1990s).

In the twentieth century, although newspapers continued to play an important role in society, communication became much easier because of the development of new forms of the media. Recent advances in science and technology allow us to transmit messages almost instantly over huge distances with television, radio and the Internet.

...eagerly awaiting the invention of the second telephone

The role of the media in society

The media has very important roles in society. Firstly, it can act as a 'gate-keeper' because it decides **what** news and issues are shown (let through the gate) and which are not.

The media can also 'set the agenda'; newspapers and television channels decide **when** and for **how long** issues are covered. (For example, the *News of the World* newspaper chose to raise the problem of naming paedophiles in England by covering related issues on the front page for a long time.) In this way, some people say that the media can create moral panics in society by encouraging people to become alarmed or panicked by an issue that they were not previously aware of.

Who owns and controls the media?

Traditionally in Britain, the media has been owned by wealthy individual families and transnational companies or multinational corporations (companies which operate in more than one country). For example, Rupert Murdoch and News International and the late Robert Maxwell and the Mirror Group. Ownership of the British press is highly **concentrated** (ie a few companies own many different types of media agencies). One such concentrated company is the Virgin Group, owned by Richard Branson.

What is the relationship between the media and politics?

It is generally accepted that newspapers can and do support particular political viewpoints and parties. This sometimes makes newspapers **biased**. Before the 1997 General Election, the *Sun* supported the Conservative Party but, just before the election, it switched sides to support New Labour. When New Labour won the election, it claimed that it was '*The* Sun *wot won it*' on the front page. The *Sun* was then the most popular national newspaper and, if you believe that the media can influence your opinions, then you can understand why the paper made such a claim. It made a similar claim in the 2001 General Election as it continued to support New Labour.

The media has also helped us find out more about the people who have been elected to represent us politically, our MPs (Members of Parliament). In recent years, the newspapers, television and the Internet have all been involved in exposing those MPs who have 'misbehaved' in some way. It can be argued that, because of the media, politicians are now more responsible to the people they are supposed to represent.

How does the media represent people?

Media images can have a powerful effect on an audience. When you think about a **stereotypical** type of person, it is often linked to the way in which the media portrays such people in

*I'm sorry Officer...
they all look the same to me!*

general. For example, think about what a typical old man looks and sounds like. Now think of a programme on television that features an 'old man', is it similar to the image you first thought of? Some women have criticised the way in which the media reinforces traditional gender stereotypes. For example, by showing women as the people who usually stay at home, look after the children and do the housework. The media can also reinforce racial stereotypes, eg by emphasising stereotypical features of black people.

Soap operas such as *Eastenders*, *Coronation Street* and *Neighbours* and 'fly-on-the-wall' television programmes about real-life situations, eg *Big Brother* and *Survivor*, are popular forms of entertainment on television. It is interesting to discuss **how** such programmes represent people in society and **why** such programmes are so popular.

Why do newspapers focus so much on the Royal Family and celebrities?

In the first half of the twentieth century, the popular press began to cut down the number of stories on political and economic matters, and increase the number of stories about sport, crime, sex, celebrities and the Royal Family. Newspapers today, particularly the tabloids, are sometimes criticised for devoting so much space to reporting stories about the lives of Royal Family members and celebrities. Yet, newspaper owners usually make a huge amount of money and are interested in printing what the public want to read in order to sell more papers. The media played a very significant role when Princess Diana died (1997) as it showed how the nation was mourning. However, sometimes people wonder why so much information is given about the intimate lives of celebrities such as 'Posh and Becks' (Victoria and David Beckham).

The Sun says that with Wills on page 1, Philip on 2, it's page 3 or nothing Ma'am!

How influential is the media?

Whether or not the media influences people is an important question. Some people say that the media has a direct effect on its audience, encouraging people to behave in certain ways. It can be said that the media is like a syringe injecting its audience with ideas that cause them to react in a certain way. For example, if a television advertisement effectively describes a brilliant new product that promises to cure baldness and someone immediately runs out and buys the product, it is possible to argue that the media has had an effect on his behaviour. Other people argue that the media does not have a direct effect on its audience, and that we are more likely to form our opinions about issues by discussing them with our family and friends.

As a citizen of this country, you have to decide what effect the media has on people, particularly the Internet, and whether the effect it has is good or bad. One issue that has been under discussion recently is the relationship between the media and violence. Is there a link between the way in which the media shows violence and people's violent behaviour? Some claim that children learn how to commit crime by seeing crimes in films and on television. An example of this was the James Bulger case in 1993, when the murder of a two-year-old child by two 11-year-old children was blamed on horror videos. One particular video, *Child's Play 3*, was generally associated with this murder, although there was no evidence that either of the children had seen it.

There are many problems in trying to prove whether or not the media causes violence, especially as some forms of violence (eg boxing) are considered to be acceptable by some but not by others.

Violence on TV

Censorship, freedom of information and the media

Censorship is the control of what people may say or hear, write or read, and see or do. The government usually exercises such control. Censorship can affect books, newspapers, magazines, films, radio, television programmes and, more recently, the Internet.

There are four major types of censorship:

- **Moral censorship** is the most common kind of censorship today, especially in England. Governments and groups try to preserve certain moral standards. Many countries, including England, have obscenity laws and these cover issues such as pornography on the Internet or in films.

- **Military censorship** is the type of censorship used during a war. Censors might cut out any information that might be valuable to the enemy. The military may also withhold information from the press for security reasons.

- **Religious censorship** occurs in some nations where the government is particularly close to one religion. Those in power may censor the ideas and practices of other religions.

- **Political censorship** – Governments that fear criticism and opposing ideas can use political censorship. This is common in non-democratic countries. In theory, democracies do not allow political censorship but many democratic governments try to discourage the expression of some radical ideas.

Freedom of the press is the right to publish facts, ideas and opinions without interference from the government or from private groups. It has been an important issue since printing began in the 1400s. Some governments across the world have taken control of the press and sometimes use it in their own interests but, usually, publishers and writers fight for as much freedom as

I know we have the right to publish facts, ideas and opinions, but why start now?

possible. Many believe that citizens need information to help them decide whether or not to support the policies of their national and local governments.

Freedom of the press exists largely in Western European countries, English-speaking nations and Japan. However, the governments of many countries continue to have strict control of the press. A number of countries in Asia, Latin America and the Middle East have censorship boards that check all publications and make sure that they follow government guidelines.

The media and the law

The Freedom of Information Act

The Freedom of Information Act (2000) provides clear rights for us to request information from what we call the **public sector** (organisations and social services run for the public). Under the terms of the Act, any member of the public will be able to apply for access to information held by organisations across the public sector.

The main features of the Act are:

- A person's right to gain access to information held by public authorities such as government departments, local authorities, health trusts, doctors' surgeries, museums and thousands of other organisations.
- The setting up of a new information commissioner and committee that has the power to make sure that people's rights are looked after.
- Stating that public authorities have a duty to publish information and make it available to people.

Some people think that this Act still does not give the media enough freedom.

Most democratic governments, like the one in Britain, limit freedom of the press in three major types of cases. This is when they believe that complete freedom of the press could endanger people, national security or social morality (the morals and values of society). Thus, they have laws against the following:

- **Libel** – insulting someone's character.
- **Sedition** – urging revolution and treason.
- **Obscenity** – offensive language.

Generally, dictatorships do not allow freedom of the press. Dictators believe that they alone hold the truth and that opposition to them endangers the country.

The British Official Secrets Act

The British Official Secrets Act (1989) forbids the leaking of confidential government material by its employees. It is an offence for a member or former member of the security and intelligence services to disclose information about their work. Journalists who write about illegally 'leaked' information might also be punished.

In many countries, there are also laws that affect press coverage of court proceedings. For example, a British newspaper may not publish comments on a trial that could prejudice the court's reputation for fairness, or publish anything that might influence the result of that trial.

Media and advertising

Most types of the media such as newspapers, television and the Internet use **advertising**. Advertisers buy space in newspapers and magazines to publish their ads and they buy time on television, radio and the Internet to broadcast their commercials.

Independent bodies, whose task it is to ensure that advertisements are legal, decent, honest and truthful, regulate advertising in the cinema, on television and on posters. There have been adverts banned or changed in some way because people believed that they were unsuitable. In the 1990s, for example, a television advert for the fizzy drink, Tango, had to be altered because it showed a man clapping another man over the ears. School children were said to be copying this in playgrounds, thus damaging each other's ears. This advert was replaced by the 'Tango man' giving another man a big kiss!

'Legal, decent, honest and truthful...'

The media, the world and 'Americanisation'

Film and television

American culture and 'the American way' has been exported by the media on a massive scale. Since the 1920s and 30s, Hollywood has dominated world film production and, in the 1970s, American films still occupied more than half of world screen time. Some people say that film and television has become too Americanised as so many films only show American culture and the American way of life. However, other countries are now starting to promote their cultures. For example, the Indian version of Hollywood, 'Bollywood', has also become popular in recent years. This produces very different types of films showing the Indian way of life.

Communication around the world

With the growth of international news, digital television, the World Wide Web and email, we are able to communicate with and learn more about each other all over the world. **Globalisation** is the term we use when we talk about how countries have become more interdependent (dependent upon each other) and this has a lot to do with the role of the media. The media is as important internationally as it is nationally. For example, the 'Internet revolution' has had a big part to play in shaping the future of the world. One issue that is currently being raised is the role of the English language. For example, most Internet sites are in English which might make information less accessible to people who do not speak English.

Questions

1. What are the roles/functions of the media?
2. How does Britain encourage freedom of information?
3. How can we check and monitor the media?

Activities

1. Find some evidence from books or the Internet to show who owns and controls newspapers. Make a list of the media companies that Rupert Murdoch owns. Explain why owning all these might be bad.
2. How do adverts portray men and women? Describe at least four examples of adverts. What are the men and women in them like? Why is this?
3. Should the Internet be censored or controlled? How could it be controlled and who do you think should be in control?
4. Imagine you are the scriptwriter for a new television soap opera. Make a list of at least five characters you would have in your soap opera. Describe what kinds of people they are.
5. Design a Web site on a topic that would be of interest to citizens across the world. How would you make that Web site accessible to everyone? What links might you include?

3 How government works

What is democracy?

Democracy is generally interpreted to mean 'people power' or 'government by the people' (Abraham Lincoln, 1863). The word democracy comes from the Greek word *demokratia* which means *demos* (people) and *kratos* (rule). **Direct democracy** is when everyone in a country votes on new laws. For example, there would be a **referendum** on every decision or new law. However, direct democracy is considered to be impossible in a lot of countries, so we have a form of **indirect democracy** or **representative government** which means that we vote for someone (a **Member of Parliament** or **MP**) to represent us when important decisions are being made.

For a country to be a representative democracy it needs to have the following characteristics:

- Everyone needs to be able to vote (we call this **universal suffrage**).
- There should be free, fair, competitive and regular **elections**.
- Only a fairly elected government should have the power to make decisions that affect the public, in other words, there should only be **government by consent**.

What do people mean by liberal democracy?

The word 'liberal' means freedom of the individual and it is usually connected with a fear of 'over-mighty' rulers. History has taught us that it is very dangerous when people, such as Hitler in Germany (1934-1945) or

Hands up all those in favour...

Stalin in the Soviet Union (1928-1953), have too much control over people's lives. In order to prevent one person or one group of people from getting too much power, we talk about a commitment to a **limited government**, eg a government that only has restricted powers.

In a **liberal democracy**, there are a variety of constraints on the government or the state's power:

- There is a **constitution**, in other words, a set of traditions and laws that limit the power of government. However, in England this constitution is not written down like it is in America, so we say that England has an **unwritten constitution** and America has a **written constitution**.

- Some countries have a **Bill of Rights** which is a set of rules guaranteeing people **human rights** (see *Chapter 1*) and what we call **civil liberties**.

- There is also the **Rule of Law** which controls government and public officials. The courts are independent and they make sure that the law is enforced. No one is above the law.

- Some countries also separate the key powerhouses of government; for example, in England we separate the Courts from the Parliament and in America they separate the President from Congress. We call this the **separation of powers** and it also helps the most powerful people in politics to 'check and balance' each other's work and prevent each other from becoming too powerful.

- Liberal democracies like France, Germany and America have lots of different **political parties** (like Labour, the Liberal Democrats and the Conservatives in England) and **interest groups** which allow people's different views to be represented. In Britain, only one party usually makes up the **Government** but **opposition** parties make sure that the Government does not have too much power.

What is the Government and what does it do?

Government is the system which rules a community. In other words, it exercises authority over people. In Britain, we elect a government to be in charge of law and order, defence, foreign affairs, trade, taxation, education, health, housing, transport, the environment, equal opportunities and many other things. The Government is usually the political party that gains the most votes in a general election.

Government has to perform three functions. It has to make law, apply or implement law and adjudicate (judge) law. We say that these three functions are carried out by three parts of government – the **legislature**, the **executive** and the **judiciary**:

Government function	Part of government	Institution
Making laws/rules	Legislature (eg to legislate is to make law)	Parliament
Applying laws/rules	Executive (eg executing a decision, administration)	Prime Minister and Cabinet supported by the civil service
Adjudicating laws/rules	Judiciary (eg to judge, interpret the law and resolve legal disputes)	The law courts

In Britain, we say that we have a 'parliamentary' system of government, whereas the USA has a 'presidential' system of government. Our Parliament is **bicameral**, this means that it is made up of two houses: the **House of Commons** and the **House of Lords** (see pages 29 and 30). In the Commons you find the main party of government (the executive branch). In the 2001 General Election, the Labour Party won more seats in the Commons than all of the other political parties put together. We therefore say that the Labour Party has the overall **majority** in the House of Commons. The leader of the Labour Party (the party with the majority) becomes the **Prime Minister** and has to appoint other members of the party to sit with him or her in the **Cabinet**.

What does Parliament do?

Parliament in the UK actually consists of the Queen, the House of Lords and the House of Commons. All three combine to carry out the work of Parliament, although when people talk about Parliament they really mean the House of Commons. Parliament has the following roles:

- It debates current affairs and makes laws.
- It examines the work of the Government on behalf of the people. They might do this by questioning or debating with the Government.
- It controls the finance, that is, the House of Commons gives permission for the Government to collect taxes and it decides how the money should be spent.
- It protects the interests and rights of individuals. We elect Members of Parliament to represent an area. These areas are known as **constituencies** (see page 40).
- It examines new proposals made by the European Union (see *Chapter 7*).

Westminster, where we find Parliament in London, is often used instead of Parliament.

What is the difference between Parliament and Government?

You find the Government inside Parliament. The Government is like the management of the country that makes the big decisions, but these decisions have to be approved by Parliament. The Government consists of approximately 100 members of the political party which has the majority of seats in the House of Commons. It prepares new policies and laws.

How does Government function in Britain?

Ministers and civil servants (the executive) usually prepare new **policies**. The policy is then presented to Parliament (the legislature) as a **Bill** which is a written document. The judiciary might be used if the policy is not put into practice.

From a Bill to an Act of Parliament

The process of taking a Bill to an Act of Parliament is as follows:

- **First Reading** – This is the formal announcement of the Bill and all its clauses by the Speaker (see page 31). The Speaker also fixes the date for the Second Reading.

- **Second Reading** – This is the stage when MPs debate the general principles of a Bill. Some modifications to the Bill can be discussed before a vote is taken. This is a crucial stage in the passage of a Bill.

- **Division** – This is when MPs vote on the aims of the Bill. If a Bill does not receive a majority of votes, it can be thrown out at this stage.

- **Committee Stage** – This is when MPs debate the finer details. MPs can propose and agree amendments to improve the Bill.

- **Report Stage** – This is when the final amended Bill is drafted and the findings of the Committee are reported back to Parliament. At the end of the Report Stage, a final Bill is drafted taking all the proposed amendments into consideration.

- **Third Reading** – This is when MPs have the opportunity to discuss and vote on the final Bill. A final vote is taken and the whole procedure is repeated in the House of Lords.

- **Royal Assent** – A Bill becomes law. The Royal Assent has not been refused since 1707.

What part of 'No' did you not understand?

FINAL BILL

A brief history of Parliament and the British constitution

- **Thirteenth century-1485** – The King (the Crown) needed information and money and so summoned representatives from local communities to create Parliament. Parliament was divided into the House of Lords and the House of Commons. It developed very basic law-making powers which limited the power of the Crown (the King or Queen).

- **1485-1688** – During Tudor times, the Monarchy had a lot of power but from 1642 to 1648 there was a Civil War which attempted to limit the power of the Crown and give more power to Parliament and the people.

So are we being civil, or is it war?

  After the Revolution of 1688, a Bill of Rights was set up and Parliament was given a lot more power.

- **1689-1832** – An independent judiciary was set up. Parliament had some control and the Monarchy no longer completely controlled the country. However, Parliament was not yet **representative** of all people because it was mostly made up of royalty and the upper classes.

- **1832 onwards** – Since 1832, there have been many changes to make the UK more **democratic**. In 1831, only the rich male property owners could vote but, by 1928, all men and women could vote (with only a few exceptions). New 'mass membership' political parties emerged which encouraged MPs to communicate more with voters and work less as individuals. A government elected by voters controlled Parliament.

However, many people still believe that Parliament is undemocratic in some ways. For example, people still think that the Queen and the Crown should not have any power at all because the people (the **electorate**) do not vote for the Monarchy. There have been many recent changes to the House of Lords because people do not like the fact that it used to be wholly made up of people who were not elected (see page 30).

What is the civil service?

Civil servants serve the elected government of the day. They are not elected and are supposed to be politically neutral, that is, they do not support one political party's ideas in particular. They are there to advise ministers on policies and to make sure that new laws and decisions are carried out.

The House of Commons and the House of Lords

The House of Commons

The House of Commons, also known as the 'Commons' or the 'Lower House', has many jobs, including examining new laws. The Commons also has a responsibility to look closely at the work of the Government. The Commons looks at the financial work of the Government and must approve Government spending and taxation (unlike the House of Lords). In practice, the Commons has much more power than the Monarch or the House of Lords.

The Commons consists of representatives who are elected by popular vote. It has 659 members, and here you find the Prime Minister and most Cabinet Ministers.

You said "Order…", Mr Speaker

The House of Commons sits for about 160 days every year from November to October. It meets in a long room called the Chamber, the famous room with rows of green benches on two sides. The Speaker of the House of Commons sits at one end of the Chamber and keeps order during debates. The MPs in the party representing the Government (the Labour Party today) sit to the right of the Speaker. The leader of the opposition and the leader of the Government (the Prime Minister) sit on the front benches opposite one another. Other members sit behind them and are known as **back-benchers**.

The House of Lords

The House of Lords, or the 'Upper House', is also part of the law-making process (legislating). It spends about two-thirds of its time revising Bills sent from the House of Commons.

The House of Lords acts as a check on the Government. For many years there has been debate about reforming the Lords because many people have criticised the fact that it is unelected by the public. The House of Lords Act 1999 stopped most of the 750 **hereditary peers** from sitting and voting in the House of Lords. In brief, the House of Lords had 1144 members until 1999, when 666 hereditary peers lost their seats and voting rights under Stage 1 of the Lords reform process. At present, 92 hereditary peers remain in the upper chamber temporarily under a deal worked out while the Government proceeds with the second stage of its reform plans. The majority of those left in place are also not elected (known as **life peers**). They are appointed by the Prime Minister, in the name of the Queen.

Who do you find in Parliament?

- **Government back-bench MPs** – MPs who belong to the same party as the Government but who do not hold a government post.
- **Opposition back-bench MPs** – MPs who belong to opposition parties and who do not hold posts in the Shadow Cabinet.
- **Official opposition** – The largest opposition party.

- **Cabinet** – This is the group of the most senior members of the Government. Members are chosen by the Prime Minister.

- **Shadow Cabinet** – This is the group of the most senior MPs from the official opposition. They 'shadow' the work of the Government.

- **Prime Minister** – The leader of the party in Government. At the moment, this is Tony Blair of the Labour Party.

- **Leader of the opposition** – The leader of the biggest opposition party (the 'official opposition'). At the moment, this is the leader of the Conservative Party, Iain Duncan Smith.

- **The Speaker of the House** – The Speaker is a neutral chairperson of debates who sits in the raised chair between the opposition and the Government.

- **Lords** – **Law lords** are chosen from among Britain's highest-ranking judges. They form the final court of appeal for civil cases throughout Great Britain and for criminal cases in England, Wales, and Northern Ireland. **Lords spiritual** are senior members of the Church of England. Life peers, law lords, and lords spiritual are appointed to their seats for life. Their children do not inherit their seats.

- **The Lord Chancellor** – This person is head of the judiciary (the law courts) and Speaker of the House of Lords. However, this person is also a member of the Government (the executive) and is appointed by the Prime Minister as a member of the Cabinet.

Oh no… Another back-bench driver

How is law enforced?

What is the state and what is society?

We use the words 'state' and 'society' in everyday language but there are many ways of interpreting what they mean. For example, the state can mean one or many nations (see *Chapter 7*), but we will take it to mean one nation here:

- **The state** – We say that the state can be a country's people, a country's territory or a country's government. A government is elected to run the state. This involves looking after properties and institutions that affect the daily lives of people who live in the country, such as hospitals, railways and social services. We say that such institutions are state-owned (ie that they belong to and are paid for by the people and run by the government).

- **Society** is usually taken to mean people who live together in any particular place or time. For example, we talk about British society or twenty-first century society. People say that some laws must be passed or enforced 'for the good of society'.

Does Parliament make all the decisions?

Power can be given to smaller communities or groups of people (such as **local governments**) and power can be given to larger groups of communities or countries (such as the **European Union**, see *Chapter 7*).

A sovereign country can conduct its own affairs, enter into **treaties** (agreements with other countries), declare war, or adopt any other course of action without another country's consent. When we talk about Britain giving up

Europe had dealt him a knockout blow...

some of its decision-making powers to larger organisations such as the European Union, some people talk about England losing her **sovereignty** (power).

The transfer of certain powers from the central government to smaller regional governments within a country is called **devolution**, as power is being devolved.

Local government

Local government generally refers to the government of an area smaller than a country such as a county or town, for example, your LEA (local education authority) is part of your local government. Local government has responsibility for the welfare of its citizens and provides certain services such as education. Elected officials or councillors run most local governments. The main functions of local government usually include road maintenance, regulation of building standards, public health, rubbish collection and looking after public facilities such as public parks.

Some people say that local authorities should have more power to make decisions about life in their communities, whilst others say they should have less.

The European Union

In 1973, Great Britain joined the European Union and, although this has brought Britain many benefits, it has also meant that Westminster (see page 26) has had to give up certain powers. For example, the European Convention on Human Rights (see page 10) has forced us to change many laws concerning working hours and human rights issues. Some people dislike being in Europe and dislike the prospect of a single European currency (the Euro), whilst others think that it is necessary for countries to work more closely together in order to progress.

Devolution: Do Scotland and Wales have their own parliaments?

Devolution is the decentralisation (taking power away from Westminster) of governmental power. The most recent examples of devolution are the setting up of the Scottish Parliament and elected Assemblies in Wales and Northern Ireland in 1998.

The National Assembly for Wales was set up as part of the process of devolution. In 1997, the Welsh people voted to set up the Assembly in a referendum. The new Assembly takes over the responsibilities of the Welsh Office and will have some law-making powers.

In 1997, the Scottish people also voted to set up the Scottish Parliament in a referendum as part of the process of devolution. The new Parliament takes on many of the responsibilities for making new laws for Scotland and has the power to vary the rate of income tax there.

What is the Northern Ireland issue?

The situation in Northern Ireland is very complicated. Hence, what is offered here is just a brief summary of the situation. Northern Ireland is part of the United Kingdom, a constitutional monarchy. There have been violent disputes between mainly Catholic groups, such as Sinn Fein and the IRA, and mainly Protestant groups,

He was delivering peace, but no one was prepared to take it...

such as the Unionists, about whether or not Northern Ireland should remain part of the UK. In 1998, the Northern Ireland Assembly was agreed by the people of Northern Ireland in a referendum as part of the devolution process and peace initiative there. The Good Friday Agreement (10 April 1998) is the latest attempt to bring peace to Northern Ireland.

Questions

1 Write definitions for all the words highlighted in bold in this chapter.

2 How is a new law made?

3 Find out the names of four members of the Cabinet. What are their roles?

4 Find out about your local MP. How do they divide their time between work in Parliament and work in their constituency?

5 Choose one of the following and describe how they work today (you may need to do some research):

- The Monarchy
- The House of Commons
- The House of Lords
- Members of Parliament
- The Prime Minister
- The official opposition
- The Cabinet
- The Scottish Parliament
- The Welsh National Assembly
- The Northern Ireland Assembly.

Activity

Produce a 'Young person's guide to Parliament' or prepare a guide to parliamentary government in the UK.

4 Political participation

In *Chapter 3*, we talked about the political system and how government works. This chapter considers how your vote or action can influence the decisions made in Westminster. Firstly, we need to consider the structure of **local government** in England, and then go on to consider **voting**, **political parties** and **pressure groups**.

What is local government?

Local government (see also page 33) generally refers to the government of an area smaller than a country, for example, the government of counties and towns in England. It is responsible for the welfare of its citizens and it is in charge of local services, such as housing or policing, and therefore can choose how to adapt these services. The local government also has to deal with complaints about these services. Although laws are made by central government at Westminster, local authorities have the freedom to shape policies to suit their local community.

Ultimately, local government allows the people of local communities to participate and have a voice in local affairs. People can do this by either standing as councillors (members of political parties) or by voting in local elections.

How much power do local governments have?

It is generally easier for people to get involved in politics at a local level but some people believe that the amount of power that local government has is very limited. This is because Britain is a **unitary** state and at the centre of the system is a parliament with sovereign power (see page 33). In other words, the local governments only get the power and money that Parliament gives them. Currently, the government department responsible for ensuring the funding and efficiency of local government is the Department of Transport, Local Government and the Regions (the DTLR). It advises local governments at all levels on issues ranging from the foot and mouth crisis to housing.

What is a general election?

A general election is when the people (the electors) vote for the candidate from the political party of their choice to be the Member of Parliament (MP) for their constituency (see page 40). The political party which wins the most seats in the House of Commons becomes the Government. In a liberal democracy (see page 24), elections allow people to decide how their country is governed. If people believe that a government or an MP is not doing his or her job then they can choose to exercise their power by not voting for them in the next election.

Election – Public vote

↓

Local MPs are elected to represent constituencies (local areas)

↓

MPs represent the people in Westminster (Parliament)

The election process in a general election

What are political parties?

It is generally assumed that a political party is a group of like-minded people organised together as a unit in order to gain power to govern a country. Every political party ultimately seeks

Seriously... it's not that sort of party!

to become the Government. The political party has to outline its particular stand on a huge range of issues. In a democracy, parties try to get power by putting forward **candidates** for election. A political party also outlines its election **manifesto** which is a list of a party's beliefs and intentions should it get into power. Issues such as the economy, tax, education, health and the European Union are addressed in an election manifesto.

In the UK, we have a **multi-party system**, that is, there are more than two parties competing for power. In contrast, America has a **two-party system** as there are only really the Democrats and the Republicans to choose from in an election; although there are people who stand as 'independents' as there are in the UK. The main three political parties in the UK at the moment are the **Conservative Party**, the **Labour Party** and the **Liberal Democrat Party**. There are also other parties that have particular influence in certain parts of the UK such as the Scottish National Party and Plaid Cymru (Wales), and there are smaller parties such as the Green Party.

Why are political parties important?

Political parties are very important because they provide the electorate with different options about how the country should be run. They are good for organising public opinion on matters that are important and they provide a permanent link between Parliament and the voters.

Anyone can form a political party but, because of our system, it is often very difficult to establish new parties. Parties need funding as, currently, they do not receive money from central government. Therefore, parties ask their members to pay membership fees and make donations.

Who can vote in a parliamentary election?

We call the right to vote the **franchise**. There have been many changes to the franchise over the years. For example, women could not vote until 1918 (and even then they had to be over 30 years old). In 1928, the Representation of the People Act gave voting rights to all men and women over the age of 21 and, in 1969, that age was reduced to 18. Today, all British citizens are entitled to register to vote as long as they are over the age of 18 and are not disqualified in any way. For example, people who are detained under mental health laws, who are sentenced to more than 12 months in prison, or who have been convicted of illegal practices during elections cannot vote.

What is a constituency?

The UK is divided up into 659 geographical areas known as **constituencies**. You register to vote in your constituency as this is where you live. The MP that you vote for will be a candidate from a particular party in your constituency.

How can people make sure that they can vote?

Although voting is not compulsory in the UK (as it is in some countries), the number of people who vote in an election says a lot about how democratic a country is. To make sure that you can vote, you have to check that you are on the **electoral register**. This is a list of all those people who have registered their right to vote in a particular constituency. Before an election, forms are sent out

Don't blame me – I didn't vote

to every householder who has to give details about everyone who lives in the house including those who will be turning 18 years of age in the next year. For the first time, the 2001 General Election allowed people to register to vote using the Internet.

Who can stand as a candidate in a general election?

In theory, anyone who is a British, Commonwealth or Irish Republic citizen may stand as a candidate at a parliamentary election as long as she or he is 21 years old or over. Those who cannot stand are more or less the same as people who cannot vote (see page 40). Other people who cannot stand as candidates are those who need to be politically neutral in their jobs, such as senior civil servants, judges, members of the police and the armed services and so forth (these people hold offices listed by the House of Commons Disqualification Act).

How often are general elections held?

Generally, an election takes place every four to five years as the maximum length of a Parliament is five years. Obviously, the Prime Minister hopes that their party is re-elected in the general election so they try to choose a time when the party is most popular in the **opinion polls**.

Date	Party, Prime Minister	Duration of government
9 June 1983	Conservative, Thatcher	4 years
11 June 1987	Conservative, Thatcher (Major 1990)	4 years, 10 months
9 April 1992	Conservative, Major	4 years, 11 months
1 May 1997	Labour, Blair	4 years, 1 month
7 June 2001	Labour, Blair	to date

Recent general election results

41

The 2001 General Election

The 1997 General Election was ground-breaking because it brought 18 years of Conservative Government to an end. Tony Blair's party, 'New Labour', gained the largest parliamentary majority of any government since 1945. The Conservative Party gained its lowest proportion of the vote since 1832 and the Liberal Democrats gained the highest number of seats (46) for a third party since 1929.

The 2001 General Election was also another landslide victory for the Labour Party:

Party	Seats won	Change from 1997
Labour	412	-6
Conservative	166	+1
Liberal Democrat	52	+6
Other	29	+1

The result was obviously good for Labour again. However, only 59.4% of those eligible to vote turned out on polling day. This was the lowest turn out since 1918. In many ways, this was in fact the lowest turn out ever because in 1918 about 60% of the electorate were newly enfranchised and not used to voting. Many men were also still in Flanders after the end of the First World War.

Facts on the 2001 General Election:

* 15% more people abstained than voted Labour.
* 17 million people did not vote; only 10.7 million voted for Labour.
* Although less than 25% of the electorate voted Labour, they won over 60% of the seats.

What is an election campaign?

Once the Prime Minister has decided to call a general election, she or he goes to see the **Monarch** (the Queen or King) to ask for Parliament to be **dissolved**. The Queen would require strong reasons to refuse because, as we know, the Monarchy does not have much power any more. The Prime

Even without campaigning, he won a clear majority

Minister announces the date of the dissolution of Parliament and the date of the general election. Election campaigns usually last for about three weeks and this is when MPs who are standing for re-election return to their constituencies as candidates hoping to be 're-elected'. Anyone else wanting to be a candidate for the election also campaigns along with the MPs seeking re-election.

Election campaigns are large, national events. Parties and candidates use the media to publicise their party messages and personalities. Election campaigns cost millions of pounds. Party leaders and senior MPs tour the country supporting local candidates and encouraging people to vote.

What is polling day?

Polling day is the day of the election; the day when the voters vote! Voters are sent **polling cards** which tell them where their nearest polling station is. Each constituency is divided into different areas (polling districts) and you find polling stations (usually schools, town halls or other public buildings) in each area.

People vote secretly and place their ballot papers in the **ballot box** (black boxes, locked and later sealed). After all the votes are in, the ballot boxes are taken to a central point in the constituency for all the votes to be counted. If the result is really close between two candidates then either candidate can demand a **recount**.

What electoral system do we use?

In a representative democracy like that in Britain, elections are a key way for the general public to participate in politics. Therefore, it is very important that the voting system we use works fairly. In England, there is a **first-past-the-post system** (FPTP). In other words, a winner-takes-all system. However, in many European countries a form of **proportional representation** (PR) is used. This is where parliamentary seats are allocated more in proportion to the amount of votes a party gets. In Scotland, for example, a mixture of FPTP and PR is used.

To be fair, I didn't win a full seat, but a small stool's a good start!

The English, first-past-the-post, system means that the candidate in a constituency with the most votes wins the election. The winning candidate only needs to get more votes than the nearest rival; they do not need more votes than all of the other candidates put together and they do not have to win more than 50% of the votes.

However, there are many people who oppose the FPTP system because they think that the result never reflects the opinion of the whole population. Instead, they think that the result should be proportional, in other words, if the Labour Party receives 44% of all the votes made then they should win 44% of the seats in the

Commons. People who would like the government to reflect public opinion more often prefer a system of proportional representation. Pressure groups (see below), such as Charter 88, campaign for a fairer election system.

Why do so few people turn out to vote?

Today, less and less people in the UK are turning out to vote at election times. For example, in the 2001 General Election, less than 60% of those eligible to vote turned out on polling day. There are lots of possible reasons for this including:

- Some people cannot vote because they failed to register in time.

- Some feel that voting is a waste of time because the result is inevitable. For example, many people did not vote in June 2001 because they thought Labour were going to win anyway and that their vote would make no difference.

- Some do not vote out of protest because they think that the voting system is undemocratic or that there is not enough choice between the parties.

- Some only vote if they feel passionate about a particular issue.

- Some are just very cynical (distrustful) or apathetic (uninterested) about politics and politicians.

I know it's important to vote – but it's raining!

Pressure groups

We can also involve ourselves in the running of the country by becoming involved in pressure groups.

What is a pressure group and how are they different from political parties?

A pressure group is an organised group (such as Amnesty International (see page 5) or Greenpeace) which aims to influence a government in some way, although they do not wish to take over power. There are thousands of pressure groups in Britain, some just act locally such as groups protesting against the building of a new road, whilst other groups are national. Some pressure groups are international, such as Amnesty International, which aims to protect individual rights across the world. The two main characteristics of pressure groups which separate them from political parties are:

- Pressure groups have **precise aims**. They might concentrate on one issue (eg children's rights), one group of people (eg old people) or one cause (eg ending homelessness). Political parties are different because they offer more general policies that cover lots of issues such as education, the economy and foreign affairs.

- Pressure groups aim to **influence governments**. Although they might be more linked to one political party than another, they only want to influence power. As we know, a political party aims to be elected so that it can govern a country. Also, sometimes, pressure groups only want to influence local councils or government agencies such as the NHS.

What are the different types of pressure groups?

There are many different types of pressure groups. However, there are two main types:

- **Promotional group** – These hope to promote an idea or cause. For example, Amnesty International campaigns for the release of political prisoners, especially those that they consider to have been unjustly treated.

- **Interest groups** – These mainly defend the interests of a particular group of people. For example, trade unions look after the interests of the workers in a common profession or industry, eg the National Union of Teachers (NUT).

How do pressure groups work?

In order to categorise the way pressure groups work we need to look at the way they seek to influence government. Groups are said to be either insider or outsider groups:

- **Insider groups** are those which work closely with the government in committees and think tanks, ie they are often consulted when important decisions are made. For example, economic organisations such as the Confederation of British Industry and trade unions sometimes work very closely with the government.

- **Outsider groups** are groups which do not consult directly with the government and seek instead to pressure the government from the outside. For example, the more radical groups such as the Animal Liberation Front uses other (sometimes illegal) methods of bringing attention to their cause.

I hate to say it, but I'm dying for a fag!

There are a range of methods used by pressure groups to influence public opinion, political parties and governments. Some of these include:

- **Lobbying** MPs and government Ministers. This means going to the entrance hall of the House of Commons or to local MPs' surgeries to present a cause or issue.

- **Advertising** in the media. Look in newspapers and you will often see advertisements from international and national pressure groups asking for money or drawing attention to their cause.

- **Leafleting** – Often, groups hand out leaflets, for example, anti-blood sports (such as foxhunting) groups are often seen in shopping areas trying to draw attention to their cause.
- Organising **petitions** or opinion polls to show how much support they have on certain issues.
- **Demonstrations** – Often, you see groups demonstrating in London outside Parliament. Recent demonstrations in the news were the 2001 May-day anti-globalisation demonstrations.
- **Civil disobedience** – This is where a group breaks the law in order to bring attention to their cause.

❓ Questions

1 How old do you have to be to vote? Can everyone in Britain vote?

2 Which political party won the last election?

3 What type of electoral (election) system do we use?

4 Why do you think so many people did not vote in the last general election? What do you think will happen to our political system if less and less people vote in elections?

5 Many more people are members of pressure groups than members of political parties. Why do you think this might be?

6 Name as many pressure groups as you can. Why do you think the number of pressure groups is growing?

⏩ Activity

Design a mock election for your school. What parties would you have standing? How would parties write their manifestos? What voting system would you adopt?

As you carry out this activity, think about this final question, if the voting age was lowered tomorrow (eg to 16 or 14 years of age), would more younger people vote?

5 How the economy works

What is the economy?

The economy is the management of money, resources, spending and saving. The economy is concerned with the production, distribution (the supply) and consumption (the use) of goods and services. In the UK, a government is elected to manage the economy carefully in order to avoid any unnecessary spending or waste.

Wants, needs and scarcity

The main problems of economics are that the wants and needs of humans are **infinite** (without limits), but resources on this earth are **finite** (limited). This means that people fear shortages of goods and services. Humans have different types of wants and needs. Economics looks only at material wants and needs. People satisfy these by consuming either **goods** (physical items such as food) or **services** (non-physical items such as heating).

Wants and needs are almost infinite because goods often need to be replaced, such as the dinner on your table or the shoes on your feet. Wants also change as new and interesting products become available and people become bored with what they already own.

Economists talk about **commodities**, which are both goods and services that are produced by using resources.

A **free good** is available without the use of resources. There is no cost, for example, for the air that we breathe. Unfortunately, we know that most things in life are not free and cost resources, eg our books need trees to be made into paper, ink and other resources before they become economic goods.

Therefore, if we now know that there are only limited resources available to produce unlimited amounts of goods and services for people, society has to make some important decisions, such as which goods and services should be made or provided. For example, do we make missiles or build hospitals and schools?

Supply and demand

Demand is the amount of a good that consumers are willing and able to buy at a given price. **Supply** is the amount of a good producers are able to sell at a given price.

Supply influences demand and demand influences supply in mixed or market economies. If there is a strong demand for Nike trainers then Nike will produce more trainers to sell. Both demand and supply will go up. However, if Nike increases the price of the trainers too much or changes to an unpopular design then the demand for Nike trainers falls. This means Nike will make less trainers.

Alternatively, if a competitor makes similar trainers and sells them at half the price, Nike will lose customers as some people will change their loyalty. Companies need to be aware of the alternative products that are being sold and their prices.

Close your eyes and choose – if you can tell the difference, I'll pay the difference

What are the different types of economic systems?

A country's **economy** is the system that decides how goods and services are provided to users. Different countries have different methods of tackling the economic problem. There are three main types of economy:

- **Market or capitalist economy** – This is a system in which most businesses are privately owned to make a profit and compete with each other. Resources are given prices without government intervention and consumers decide the type and quantity of goods to be bought. The US and Hong Kong are examples of market economies where firms decide the type and quantity of goods to be made in response to consumers. People who earn a lot can buy more goods and services than the less well off.

- **Command economy** – In a command-planned or socialist economy, local or national government owns most businesses, and there is little or no competition. The government owns most resources and decides on the type and quantity of goods, to be made. The former Soviet Union and North Korea are examples of command economies. Incomes are often more evenly spread out than in other types of economy and there is less inequality.

- **Mixed economy** – This is a system in which businesses are owned both privately and by the state. The UK economy is a mixed economy. This means that it has a **public sector** and a **private sector**. In a mixed economy, private firms make goods, while the government organises the distribution of basic goods, and services such as education and health care.

The economy of a country may depend upon some of the following factors:

- **The population** – In order for a government to plan which goods and services are needed, information about the population is required. The study of the population is called **demography**. Since 1801, a population census (survey) of the UK has been made every ten years to count the number of people in the country. A census is carried out because the government needs to plan ahead. The figures can be used to estimate, for example, the number of roads, schools or hospitals likely to be needed in the future.

- **The birth rate** – The birth rate is the number of births per thousand of the population in a year. The birth rate fell dramatically from 1900 to 2000 due to the following:
    - Improved birth control – Contraceptives are now more available and socially accepted.
    - Women choosing to continue working, or waiting before raising smaller families.
- **The death rate** – The death rate is the number of deaths per thousand of the population in a year. The death rate in the UK has fallen from 18.4 in 1900 to 11.7 in 1988. This fall has been caused by:
    - Improved housing, diet and sanitation.
    - Improved health care through medical discoveries and the National Health Service (NHS).

She's busy... can you come back later?

- **Migration** – Migration happens when people leave a country (emigration) or enter it (immigration). This affects the size of the population. Net migration is the difference between the number of people emigrating and immigrating. People usually leave countries for two reasons:
  - **Push factors** – These include high unemployment, low living standards or poor climate at home.
  - **Pull factors** – These include good job prospects and high living standards in a new country.

The public sector

The economy can be divided into private and public sectors. The **public sector** is made up of organisations that are either the responsibility of central or local government. For example, in the UK, the Government is responsible for the National Health Service, the emergency services, the armed forces and state education. Central government controls these organisations. Their main aim is to provide essential services for the whole population. These organisations are non-profit making and the general public pays for these services through **taxation** (see *Chapter 6*).

There are several advantages for society of public ownership:

- The main argument is that the whole population benefits from the goods and services produced rather than just those who can afford to pay for them. Essential services like health and education are provided for everyone. Before the creation of the NHS, you had to pay to see a doctor. Today, we pay through taxation, but those who earn less, pay less and the unemployed are provided for.
- As trade unions can protect jobs, unemployment is reduced in state-owned enterprises. Resources and supplies, such as water and energy, can be guaranteed and channelled to the areas that need them most.

Disadvantages for society of public ownership include:

- The main argument against public ownership is its cost. More public services mean a higher tax bill for everybody, including those who may not benefit from them.
- Also, large public sector organisations are often bureaucratic. They often have a monopoly (little competition from other organisations) and, without competition, workers can be less motivated and this can lead to inefficiency.

What are public corporations?

The state rather than shareholders own public corporations. The government makes policy, and ensures they perform their functions properly. Much of the money comes from the Treasury, through taxation or grants. The relevant government Minister can influence the choice of a corporation's board and chairperson. Each Minister is responsible for how money is spent in their department and can be questioned in Parliament.

Parliamentary committees are set up to deal with any complaints about public corporations. Despite this, corporations have a separate identity and their board controls the everyday running of the organisation.

The BBC, for example, has its own board, but is answerable to the government. It is largely funded through the TV licence fee, collected by the Treasury. Questions are asked in the House of Commons about how the BBC spends taxpayers' money and the Minister for Culture, Media and Sport answers.

The private sector

The aim of a business in the **private sector** is to survive by making a profit. This may be a sole trader working alone, like a newsagent, or thousands of shareholders in a large public limited company. In the private sector, individuals (shareholders, sole traders or partners) own businesses.

What is privatisation?

During the 1980s, the British Government decided to **privatise** most of the nationalised (publicly owned) industries believing that the added competition and profit motive would improve efficiency and provide a better value-for-money service for the consumer. Examples include British Gas, British Airways and British Telecom (now BT).

Arguments for privatisation include:

- Firms are more efficient in the private sector because they are trying to make profits.
- Money can be raised to increase government services or pay for tax cuts.
- Ordinary people become shareholders and take a greater interest in economic matters.

Arguments against privatisation include:

- Public monopolies simply become private monopolies.
- Socially necessary but unprofitable services may not now be provided.
- Nationalised industries are already owned indirectly by the general public.

Multinational corporations

A multinational corporation is a big firm with a head office in one country and several branches in other countries. McDonalds, Coca-Cola and Nike are examples of multinational corporations.

People have mixed feelings about whether or not multinational companies benefit developing countries. Different companies have different policies. A multinational company can create jobs for the country that they move to, known as the host country. Often, the company will introduce new production techniques and managerial skills. Sometimes, new or better goods may become available in the host country and workers are paid more than they would be in other jobs.

However, there are also problems with some multinational companies. Often, profits that are made are returned to the overseas head office so they do not benefit the host country. Also, the multinational may do something against the interest of the host country such as creating unwanted pollution. A multinational may force its overseas branches to buy resources from home and not from the host country. Some multinationals know they can get cheap labour if they set up factories overseas and, as there is no **minimum wage**, they can pay workers less. Multinationals can also avoid certain taxes if they operate abroad.

Why are multinational corporations criticised?

Multinational corporations are often under pressure from groups protesting about their business practices or political involvement. There are often ethical campaigns from pressure groups (see page 45). Coca-Cola advertisements often show American teenagers saying 'It's the Real Thing' and 'I'd like to buy the world a Coke'. Recently, Coca-Cola urged us to 'Think globally, Act locally'. But the 'Think globally' slogan is used by environmentalists to stress the importance of the individual in protecting the planet. However, the Coca-Cola company made a $1m donation to the presidential campaign of George W Bush and some people argue that Bush is environmentally unfriendly. For example, Bush did not agree to the Kyoto Treaty on global warming, which had given the US until 2012 to reduce its carbon dioxide emissions by 7% from their 1990 levels. Yet, by 2000, US emission levels had actually risen by 10%.

Trust me, George... It'll work!

Environmentalists were upset about Bush's actions. In the UK, a group of MPs launched a campaign aimed at Coca-Cola. The MPs hoped that young people would email the UK offices of Coca-Cola and the White House to express their concern.

In 1995, consumers were asked to boycott French products in protest at the French Government's nuclear tests in the South Pacific. However, shoppers found it hard to link the piece of Brie in their shopping basket with the stopping of nuclear testing in France.

Are you sure this is Brie?

Government income, spending and borrowing

Why does the Government need money?

The Government needs money to pay for public services and goods. This money, known as **revenue**, can be raised through taxation, national insurance contributions, borrowing, charging for services or by selling state-owned assets.

What is taxation?

People pay **tax** to the Government to pay for **Government spending**. Tax can also help redistribute income from the rich to the poor: you pay more tax if you earn more and still receive the same public services and goods as those who do not earn as much.

Taxes need to be defined so that everyone knows the amount, method and time of payment. A tax should be **equitable** (fair). A tax should not be too high or act as a **disincentive** to stop people from working. Taxes also need to be flexible so that the Government can use tax changes to help control the economy.

The main types of taxation are:

- **Income tax** (or direct tax) – This is a tax on your earnings; people pay more if they earn more. Usually, this is paid directly to the Inland Revenue.
- **Value added tax** (VAT) is a tax on spending – 17.5%, for example, is added onto the selling price of many goods and services.
- **Duties** are taxes on the sale of luxury goods – A set amount is added to the selling price.
- **Council tax** is a local tax on property – All properties are valued and the amount of council tax paid depends on the **value band** that the property falls into and the area in which a person lives.
- **Corporation tax** is a tax that a company pays and depends on profits.
- **Inheritance tax** is a tax on the transfer of money and property.

How can people influence taxation?

Citizens can influence how much tax local and national governments raise, and what they spend it on. They can do this by voting in elections (see *Chapter 4*), by forming and supporting pressure groups or joining groups of protesters.

In September 2000, there were mass protests at the rising prices on fuel leading to several days of disruption caused by protestors blockading the country's refineries and oil depots. Truck drivers protesting against high fuel prices converged on London and other cities, and blocked motorways. This caused the Labour Government to meet with executives of oil companies and review the escalating prices.

What is the Budget?

The **Chancellor of the Exchequer** is the Minister of Finance in charge of the Treasury. The Chancellor announces how much the Government is going to spend over the next 12 months in what is called the **Budget**. The Government states how it is going to raise the money to pay for its expenditure at the same time.

How does the Government spend money?

The Government spends money on providing public goods and services and aims to relieve poverty. Examples of public goods include street lighting, roads and transport.

What is inflation?

Inflation refers to the continual increase in prices. The value or buying power of money refers to the amount of goods or services one pound can buy. Inflation means the value of money is falling because prices keep rising.

Sorry... It's inflation!

 Questions

1 What influences the price of a good in the shops?

2 What type of economy do we have in the UK?

3 How does the UK economy differ from a command economy?

4 What is the study of the population called?

5 Why is it useful to learn about the population?

6 Should the NHS be run by the Government or by private companies? What reasons do you have for your answers?

7 Do you think that not buying a good because we disagree with the policies or ethics of a company is a good idea? Why?

6 Employment and money

Employment

People who make their living by working for someone else or a company (known as an **employer**) are called **employees** because they are in employment. Those who make their living by providing goods and services without working for an employer are known as **self-employed**. If people lose their jobs and are unable to find paid work, they are known as **unemployed**.

Employers and employees have rights protected by law. Since 1994, both part-time and full-time employees have the same rights. Employment rights include:

- Employees are protected by **disability, race and sex discrimination laws**.
- Employees have to be given notice if they are asked to leave once they have worked for more than a month. After two months, employees should receive the **terms and conditions** of their jobs in writing.
- Employees are entitled to **redundancy pay** if they are made redundant and have worked for the employer for two years or more.
- Employees are able to claim for **unfair dismissal** if they have worked for an employer for at least a year and feel that they have been unfairly sacked.
- All employees aged 18 or over are entitled to receive at least the **minimum wage** which is £3.50 per hour (£4.10 for employees aged 22 years and over).
- An employer must make sure that the **workplace is safe** as the employer has a legal responsibility to follow all safety procedures.
- All employees over the age of 16 have the right to at least four weeks' **paid holiday** a year as long as they have worked for at least 13 weeks.

How old do you have to be to work?

Children aged 14 or over can be employed in light work only. Those under 14 years of age can only be given very light work such as paper rounds that are supervised by a parent. If you are under school leaving age, you cannot work before 7 am or after 7 pm, and you should not work for more than two hours on a school day.

NEEE–NORR...
NEEE–NORR...

Is it me... or are policemen getting younger?

What are apprenticeships?

Modern apprenticeships or traineeships are a form of training for people who wish to follow careers such as being a technician, accountant, junior manager or craftsman. You receive some pay (at least £40 per week, although the minimum wage does not always apply to apprenticeships) whilst you are trained.

What should the 'terms and conditions' tell you?

Terms and conditions should tell you about how you are going to be trained, your pay, the date you began to work and your working hours. It should also contain details about sick pay and pensions, information about the company's disciplinary procedures and the amount of notice you need to give if you wish to leave. If you are at all concerned about your terms and conditions, or about equal opportunities in your job, you should visit the local Citizens Advice Bureau or your careers office at school.

What should be in a contract?

All employees should have a contract. This is the agreement between a worker and an employer. The contract explains working hours, pay, holiday entitlement, how much notice has to be given if either side wishes to end the employment and a job description (the sort of job the employee is to do). The contract can be part of the terms and conditions. A contract is usually in writing but it can be agreed verbally.

What is the Disability Discrimination Act?

The Disability Discrimination Act was passed in 1995 to protect certain groups of disabled people from unfair discrimination. It only applies to companies that have more than 20 employees. It states that it is unfair to treat a disabled person less favourably than anyone else. It also states that companies should make sure that the workplace is adjusted for disabled people, for example, by having ramps and disabled toilets. This law also applies to trainees.

Trade unions and strikes

A strike is a situation when the employees wish to pressure their employer to change working conditions or increase their pay. Often, employees are members of a **trade union**. This is an organisation which exists to protect the rights of workers. If there was a case of unfair dismissal (being sacked or made redundant from a job unfairly), a union would defend their workers and possibly take the employer to a tribunal or court.

Trade unions aim to:

- improve the pay of workers
- improve working conditions and secure longer holidays
- protect members' jobs
- provide local, social and welfare facilities
- influence government policy by sponsoring MPs and giving money to political parties.

Workers' rights and discrimination

What are maternity rights?

If employees are pregnant, they are entitled to at least 18 weeks' **maternity leave**. Maternity allowance is available from the Benefits Agency for those who are on a low income or who have not worked for long enough to qualify for maternity pay. Both parents are entitled to 13 weeks' unpaid parental leave in the first five years of their child's life.

Sorry Bob, I know it's exceptional circumstances, but it clearly says maternity leave...

How can people be discriminated against at work?

If someone is not treated as well as someone else because of their sex, race, etc, it is called **direct discrimination**. It is against the law for an employer to discriminate against someone because of their marital status, disability, sex, race, colour or nationality. Four laws protect people from discrimination:

- **The Equal Pay Act** (1970) – Many women who did exactly the same job as men got paid less just because of their sex until this Act came into force.

- **The Sex Discrimination Act** (1975) – Sexual harassment is when people feel that they are receiving unwanted physical contact or being victimised because of their sex.

- **The Race Relations Act** (1976) – This protects people who feel that they have been discriminated against because of their race.

- **The Disability Discrimination Act** (1995) – See page 62.

What happens if someone is sacked unfairly?

If someone loses their job and feels that they have been unfairly treated and they have worked for an employer for a year or more, a complaint can be made to the employment tribunal. An employer cannot sack an employee without giving them the notice stated in the contract unless an employee has committed **gross misconduct**. Gross misconduct might be extremely bad behaviour such as theft.

People are also entitled to **redundancy pay** if they have worked for their employer for at least two years since they were 18 and have not turned down another job offer from their employer.

Can people in the UK work anywhere?

If you are British, you can work anywhere in the UK or in the European Union. By being a member of the EU, British citizens have the right to live and work anywhere in the EU. It is also possible to work in non-European Union countries but you will probably need a **work permit** and **visa**.

Unemployment

We say that the UK population divides into two types:

- The **working population** is made up of people of working age who are available to work. It does not include people in full-time education. All people employed or self-employed make up the labour force (workforce).
- **Dependants** make up the rest of the population.

How can we measure unemployment?

When calculating the level of unemployment, the Government only counts those people who register as unemployed and claim benefit. A large number of people seeking work either do not register or do not claim benefit and are, therefore, not included in the official figures. The **unemployment rate** is the percentage of the labour force **officially** jobless. **Full employment** is when there are more job vacancies than unemployed people.

Income, money and banking

What is income?

Income is the amount of money received by a household or person over time. This may come from employment, self-employment, rent or other sources. Income distribution is the way in which this is shared out between households. Not everyone receives the same amount of money each year because of **wage differences** and differences in wealth. Workers sell their labour to employers in return for **salaries** that are paid monthly or **wages** that are paid weekly.

What money can you take home?

The **gross wage** per year is made up of your wages plus any extra hours you work (**overtime**) and any bonuses you receive. However, you cannot take all this home as taxes are then paid in the form of income tax and national insurance contributions. The rest is called **net wages** or take-home pay.

Wage differences: Who decides how much you earn?

In a market economy (see page 51), the wage for a job is determined by the supply and demand for labour in that particular occupation. A job where labour is in high demand but in short supply will pay higher wages.

Sometimes, workers in the same industry doing the same job may be paid different amounts. A **wage drift** occurs when the earnings of some workers rise above average. This happens for several reasons. It may be that workers in cities are sometimes paid more to meet the higher costs of living. Also, in spite of equal opportunities laws, women tend to earn less. Older workers tend to earn more because they are paid a bonus to reward experience. Some workers are paid more for working harder and some get money in overtime.

What do we mean by the standard of living?

The value of this year's national income is a useful measure of how well off a country is. The **standard of living** refers to the amount of goods and services consumed by households in one year. A high standard of living means households consume a large number of goods and services. An increase in ownership of luxuries such as cars, televisions, etc, shows an improved standard of living.

Money and banking

What is the history of money?

The earliest method of exchange was **bartering**, where goods were exchanged directly for others. Problems arose when someone did not want what was being offered in exchange for the other good, or if no agreement could be reached over how much one good was worth.

Valuable metals such as gold and silver began acting as a **medium of exchange**. Governments decided to melt these into coins. By the seventeenth century, people were leaving gold with the local goldsmith for safekeeping. Receipts of £1 and £5 were issued which could then be converted back into gold at any time. Soon these receipts were recognised as being 'as good as gold' and were taken in exchange for goods. Goldsmiths became the first bankers and their receipts became banknotes.

What's the exchange rate for chickens?

Today, only the Bank of England can issue banknotes in England and Wales (see below). (In Scotland, however, three banks can issue banknotes – The Bank of Scotland, The Royal Bank of Scotland and Clydesdale Bank.) However, notes are not usually used to buy expensive items. The buyer is more likely to write out a cheque, which instructs his or her bank to transfer money from their account into the account of the seller, or use a credit card. The main function of money now is as a medium of exchange for buying goods and services.

But I can't be overdrawn – I've still got cheques left!

What are commercial banks?

Banks such as Lloyds or Barclays are authorised institutions and they perform four main functions. They accept deposits, make loans, arrange payment of bills and provide customer services.

What is the Bank of England?

The Bank of England, established in 1694, is the central bank of the UK and is the sole issuer of notes and coins through the Royal Mint. It is also the Government's banker and holds the UK gold in a special account.

What is the Stock Exchange?

The London Stock Exchange provides large-scale long-term loans for companies and the Government.

Firms can raise money by arranging a loan through a bank. However, a company may consider going public and become a public limited company to raise more money. The firm invites the public to buy **shares**. If the company does well and makes a profit, shares will increase in value and the people who own the shares (shareholders) can exchange them for money. An increase in the demand for a share will raise its price. This may be the result of increased profits or a good economy.

 Questions

1 What are trade unions?

2 What are employment rights? Can you name a few?

3 What makes people go on strike? Can you think of a reason why your teachers may decide to go on strike?

4 What laws are there to help us if we are discriminated against (treated unfairly) at work?

5 What influences the amount of money a person earns for his or her job?

6 When you earn an income, can you take all of the money you earn home? What happens to your money?

7 The European Union

Map showing all EU
Member States

It is important for you to understand the following key words before you read this chapter:

- **Member State** – A country which has joined the European Union (EU).
- **Economic** – Financial, related to money.
- **Political** – Related to government, politics and making laws.
- **Treaty** – An agreement or contract between the members of the EU.

What is the European Union?

The European Union is an international body which directly affects the lives of 375 million citizens. It stretches from Western Europe, bordered by the Mediterranean Sea to the south, Atlantic and Arctic Oceans to the west and north and reaches the countries of Central and Eastern Europe.

What is the European Union for?

The EU was originally created so that its Member States would become one big market where people and companies could work as though they were in one single country. It was hoped that closer links between countries could prevent war and make Europe stronger. To achieve this Single Market, four freedoms were identified to be essential requirements – the free movement of:

- **Products** – People can sell and buy goods anywhere in the EU.
- **People** – In theory, every citizen is able to live and work anywhere in the EU.
- **Services** – Service providers, such as holiday companies, can operate under the same conditions anywhere in the EU.
- **Capital (money)** – Money can move freely throughout the EU and people can, in theory, keep money wherever they want.

What are my rights as a citizen of the European Union?

Being part of the EU entitles citizens to certain rights. EU citizenship was introduced in the **Maastricht Treaty** (1992) and it was clarified in the 1997 Treaty of Amsterdam that EU citizenship goes together with national citizenship and does not replace it. Rights for members of the EU include the right to:

- travel, live, work and study in any Member State
- vote in local and European Parliament elections in country of origin or residence
- petition to the President of European Parliament on EU matters
- diplomatic protection, in other words, a citizen of the EU is entitled to the same protection as nationals of other Member States.

Countries have to meet certain requirements to join the EU. Some questions to ask when reading about the EU include: Do citizens of countries outside the EU feel discriminated against? Is there a two-tier Europe – one with countries of the EU and one with poorer countries?

What is the history of the EU?

In spring 1950, Europe was very fragile. With the start of the Cold War (see page 110), the threat of conflict between East and West threatened the continent (the geographical area of Europe). Five years after the Second World War ended, old enemies, France and Germany were still not getting along, having been at war on and off since the 1870s. To create conditions for a lasting peace, a link had to be made between the two.

Can we stop now – I'm freezing!

At first, a European Coal and Steel Community (ECSC), was formed in April 1951 and its members were France, Germany, Italy, the Netherlands, Belgium and Luxembourg. *'We are not building a coalition of States, we are uniting people,'* wrote Jean Monnet (see http://www.jean-monnet.net/).

Under pressure from the Cold War, the six Member States decided to improve the economy by setting up a **Common Market**. The Treaty of Rome of 25 March 1957 established the **European Economic Community** (EEC). This involved the setting up of decision-making bodies that enabled Member States to express their views, needs and concerns.

Between 1958 and 1970, the abolition of **customs duties** meant countries could trade more freely with each other. Increased trade meant that living standards rose. Since trade has become easier, consumers have become used to seeing an ever-increasing variety of imported goods in shops. In 1995, the 15 EU countries and 12 countries with coastlines on the southern Mediterranean established a partnership and set up a free-trade area.

Treaty on European Union

When the Treaty on European Union (the Maastricht Treaty) came into force, it gave European integration a new dimension. The European Community, which was mainly an economic union, transformed into a European Union, which we say is now based on three pillars:

- The **community pillar** directs how the Commission, Parliament, the Council and Court of Justice work. Basically, it manages the economic market and common policies (eg deciding what all the countries' policies on agriculture or food quality are).
- **Foreign and security policy** – This pillar deals with how Member States treat other countries and how they protect themselves together from outside threats.
- **Justice and home affairs** – This pillar covers matters such as immigration and asylum policy, the police and justice.

What is the economic and monetary union (EMU)?

The main thing people remember about the Maastricht Treaty is the decision to move towards economic and monetary union (EMU). This involves replacing currencies of individual Member States with a single currency, the Euro.

I can't wait to hear you explain this!

The introduction of the single currency is a big step as there are consequences for each citizen. Eleven of the 15 EU Member States adopted the Euro as a common currency (known as **Euro zone**). Three Member States (Denmark, Sweden and the UK) did not join, although they can join later if they wish.

On 1 January 2002, banknotes and coins denominated in Euros were circulated in the participating Member States, alongside the banknotes and coins in national currencies.

What issues face the EU at the start of the twenty-first century?

Security and defence

The Treaty on European Union sets aims and procedures for a Common Foreign and Security Policy (CFSP), with the idea that it could lead to a **common defence policy**, where all states would agree how best to defend the combined territory of the Member States combined. But nations still have to work hard if they are to agree how to best protect themselves. It will be up to Member States to decide how much national power they want to give up to create a joint power.

Enlargement

Membership of the EU is open to any country in Europe that wants to join and can take on the commitments made in the Treaties. There are two conditions that determine whether a country can join:

- The country must be in Europe.
- The country must apply democratic procedures under the rule of law.

Denmark, Ireland and the UK became members in 1973. Later, in the 1980s, southern members such as Greece, Spain and Portugal were admitted. The third wave, in 1995, allowed Austria, Sweden and Finland to join.

Current EU enlargement policy is concerned with increasing the size of the EU by admitting further countries. These countries need to work towards meeting the following conditions for entry:

- Respect for democratic principles, the rule of law and human rights.
- Creation of a market economy.

There are currently 13 applicant countries: Bulgaria, Cyprus, the Czech Republic, Estonia, Hungary, Latvia, Lithuania, Malta, Poland, Romania, the Slovak Republic, Slovenia and Turkey. In 1998, it was decided to start negotiating conditions to join with Cyprus, the Czech Republic, Estonia, Hungary, Poland and Slovenia.

Decision-making in the EU

There are three main bodies responsible for legislation in the EU. The Council of the European Union (often referred to as the Council of Ministers), the European Parliament and the European Commission.

The Council of the European Union (Council of Ministers)

The Council of Ministers is the supreme law-making body of the EU as it adopts and decides which laws will be enforced in every

Member State. It consists of ministers from the 15 Member States, each representing national interests and issues.

The Presidency of the Council determines the Council's priorities, and sets the agenda. The position rotates every six months among the Member States.

European Parliament

EU citizens elect the European Parliament every five years. Currently, there are 626 Members of the European Parliament (MEPs). They are elected directly in each Member State. The UK had its last European Election in the year 2000. Europe's citizens elect members to sit in multinational parliamentary groups, parties that have broadly the same interests but have members from different countries.

The European Parliament has the following powers:

- **Legislation (making laws/rules)** – The right to be consulted, amend legislation (laws) proposed by the Commission, delay or reject legislation and issue reports.
- **Finance (organise the money)** – The right to change certain items of spending and reject the Community budget.
- **Control** – The right to question the Council and Commission and monitor their work.

The Parliament meets in Strasbourg every month apart from August. Recently, powers of the Parliament have grown and the European Parliament often makes joint decisions with the Council.

The European Commission

The European Commission is like a civil service for the EU, taking care of the day-to-day running of the organisation. There are 20 Commissioners, each with responsibility for a policy area, for example, enlargement, agriculture, etc.

The Commission proposes legislation (new bills and laws) to the Council of Ministers and the European Parliament and is responsible for making sure Member States apply the Treaties properly. It can take institutions or Member States before the Court of Justice.

What is the European Court of Justice?

The Court of Justice in Luxembourg consists of 15 judges and eight advocates-general, appointed for six years. One judge represents each Member State.

The Court is usually seen as the last resort for deciding legal decisions. It judges Member States, institutions and companies which are said to have broken EU law. It also deals with complaints about EU law.

The EU and international relations

When we talk about international relations, we usually include the following areas: defence, aid (support), peace, promoting cooperation and environmental issues. The EU has a strong international dimension. It often attempts to improve or develop relationships with other non-member countries and international organisations. Other aims include:

- **Peace** – The twenty-first century will see a Europe aim to assert itself as a force for peace, after being at the heart of two world wars in the twentieth century. The Union also has to work hard to encourage stability and development within the regions that surround it.

Now let's hope it sticks!

- **Overseas aid and development** – The European Community Humanitarian Office (ECHO) provides emergency assistance and relief to victims of natural disasters or armed conflict outside EU. The aim is to provide aid to disaster zones quickly. Aid may consist of food, medicines, other essential supplies or personnel. For example, the ECHO may finance humanitarian landmine clearance operations and provides information for people in affected areas about the dangers of landmines.

What is development aid?

Community development cooperation policy aims to help development and combat poverty in developing countries and integrate them into the world economy. The EU tries to promote the rule of law and respect for human rights. Aid programmes are organised on a regional basis (eg in African states or Latin America) and also by themes (eg food, aid, environment or health).

 Questions

1 Should the EU enlarge? Why? Why not? What might have to change if more countries were to join?

2 Will a larger EU mean less democracy?

3 When would a decision made at EU level be more effective than one made in a Member State alone? Think of crime, environment, farming, etc.

4 Why might some countries not like important issues to be discussed on a larger scale?

8 The United Nations

What is the United Nations?

The United Nations (UN) is an organisation of independent countries that joined together to work for world peace and fight poverty and injustice. It was created on 24 October 1945 and 51 Member States signed up. United Nations Day is celebrated on 24 October each year. Currently, the UN has 189 Member States.

In 1945, President Roosevelt met with Winston Churchill (Prime Minister of the UK) and Joseph Stalin (leader of the Soviet Union) to work out a way to prevent another world war. They decided to form the UN, an organisation of all the countries in the world to prevent a world war happening ever again.

A **Charter** was drawn up by the countries at the UN Conference on International Organisation in 1945. It is a treaty which sets out basic principles for international relations. The Charter was signed on 26 June 1945 by representatives of 50 countries. Poland signed later.

How does the United Nations work?

When states become members of the United Nations, they agree to accept the rules of the UN Charter.

Believe me, it's best you come to an UNderstanding!

According to the Charter, the UN has four purposes:

- Keeping peace throughout the world.
- Developing friendly relations between nations.
- Helping improve living conditions of the poor and encouraging respect for others' rights and freedoms (including getting rid of poverty, disease, environmental destruction and illiteracy).
- Being a centre for uniting nations to achieve these aims.

The UN is not a world government and it does not make laws. It does, however, provide the means to help resolve international conflict and create policies on matters that affect us all. At the UN, all the Member States – large and small, rich and poor, with differing political views and social systems – have a voice and vote in this process.

How are decisions made in the UN?

Decision-making within the UN system is not easy. This is because the UN is made up of many different independent states, each with their own views. This means that before an action can be carried out, it has to be agreed and funded by all Member States. In matters of **peace-keeping** and international politics, it requires a difficult, often slow, process of **consensus-building** (creating agreements that everyone is happy with) that must take into account national as well as global needs. A lot of people believe this to be a problem as important decisions can take many years to be reached and the process of decision-making is therefore very slow.

How does the UN affect our lives?

The UN affects our lives in several ways:

- The UN is central to global efforts to solve the bigger problems that challenge humanity (all people).
- Every day, the UN and its family of organisations work to promote respect for human rights, protect the environment, fight disease, promote development and reduce poverty.

- The UN leads international campaigns against drug trafficking and terrorism. Throughout the world, the UN and its agencies help **refugees** and set up programmes to clear landmines, improve the quality of drinking water and increase food production. The UN also lends money to developing countries.

What is the UN system?

The UN has six main parts. Five of them – the General Assembly, the Security Council, the Economic and Social Council (ECOSOC), the Trusteeship Council and the Secretariat – are based at the UN Headquarters in New York. The sixth, the International Court of Justice, is located at The Hague in the Netherlands. A number of UN offices, programmes and funds, such as the Office of the UN High Commissioner for Refugees (UNHCR), the UN Development Programme (UNDP) and the UN Children's Fund (UNICEF), also work to improve the economic and social condition of people around the world.

The General Assembly

The General Assembly is a kind of world parliament of nations where all Members of the UN meet to discuss and make suggestions on subjects they consider important. It meets once a year for about three months.

During the 2000/2001 sessions, the Assembly considered more than 170 different topics, including globalisation, nuclear disarmament, development, protection of the environment and the addition of new democracies.

In the General Assembly, most decisions need a simple majority (over 50%), others require a two-thirds majority. Each country, large or small, rich or poor, has one vote, unlike the Council of Ministers in the European Union, where votes are weighted depending on population. China, with over a billion citizens, has one vote, as has Palau, the smallest UN country, with only 17 000 citizens.

Although Member States cannot be forced to carry out decisions made by the Assembly, the Assembly's decisions have a great impact on all Member States.

The Security Council

The Security Council's job is to maintain international peace and security. The Council may meet at any time, day or night, if peace is threatened. All the UN Member States have agreed to accept the decisions of the Security Council.

The Security Council has 15 members. Five of these – China, France, the Russian Federation, the United Kingdom and the United States – are **permanent members**. The other ten **non-permanent members** are elected by the General Assembly every two years. Member States are talking about changing the Security Council's membership to reflect today's political and economic realities.

Decisions of the Council require nine 'Yes' votes. But a decision cannot be taken if there is a 'No' vote, or **veto**, from a permanent member.

During the Cold War (1945-1990), the Soviet Union often rejected decisions made by the US, and vice versa. This meant that the Security Council was often unable to act.

In the event of a war, the Council tries to get a **ceasefire** (where both sides agree to stop military

How about we settle this with a game of Twister?

action or fighting). A **peacekeeping mission** may be sent to help keep peace and keep opposing forces apart. The Council can enforce its decisions in a number of ways. It can call for **economic sanctions**, where trade is stopped with the country that is not being peaceful, or order an **arms embargo**, where arms are not allowed in to a country. Sometimes, the Council lets Member States use 'all necessary means', including military action, to see that its decisions are carried out.

The Economic and Social Council

The Economic and Social Council (ECOSOC) deals with economic problems such as poverty, the environment and trade. ECOSOC plays a key role in helping international cooperation for development. It is concerned with social issues such as population, the condition of women and children, housing, racial discrimination, crime, youth and food, and makes suggestions on how to improve education and health conditions.

ECOSOC talks with non-governmental organisations (NGOs), linking the UN to people. It has 54 members, elected by the General Assembly for three-year terms. It meets yearly, so that Ministers can discuss major economic and social issues.

It works with specialised agencies which are part of the UN 'family'. The UN itself also has departments and programmes, for example, UNDP.

It makes programmes to improve working conditions and employment opportunities, and sets labour standards for countries around the world. It works to improve agricultural productivity and food security, and to better the living standards of rural populations.

ECOSOC promotes education for all, cultural development, protection of the world's natural and cultural heritage, international cooperation in science and freedom of speech. It also organises a programme to solve health problems. It works in areas such as immunisation (protection from diseases), health education and providing basic drugs.

The Trusteeship Council

When the UN began, some countries were not free to form their own government. These places had UN protection and were called the 11 Trust Territories. The Trusteeship Council was set up to help these countries to form their own governments. By 1994, all Trust Territories achieved independence, either as states or by joining neighbouring independent countries.

The Secretariat

The people who work in the headquarters in New York and UN offices in Geneva, Vienna and Nairobi and in offices all over the world form the Secretariat and carry out the administrative work of the UN. These people are known as international civil servants. The most senior person is the **Secretary-General**; Kofi Annan from Ghana at the moment. The Secretariat consists of departments and offices with a total staff of about 8900, drawn from some 160 countries.

The International Court of Justice

The International Court of Justice, also known as the World Court, hears complaints and passes judgement. Only countries and not individuals can take cases before this court. It sits in The Hague in the Netherlands and has 15 judges elected by the General Assembly and the Security Council. If a state agrees to participate, it has to obey the Court's decision.

What does the UN do to keep the peace?

Keeping world peace is a central purpose of the UN. Member States agree to settle disputes by peaceful means and avoid threatening or using force against other states.

Over the years, the UN has helped defuse international crises and resolve conflicts. It has taken on big operations involving peacekeeping and humanitarian assistance. It has worked to prevent conflicts from breaking out. In post-war situations, it tries to help lay the foundations for lasting peace.

For example:

- In 1988, a UN-run peace settlement ended the Iran–Iraq war, and, in the following year, UN-sponsored negotiations led to the withdrawal of Soviet troops from Afghanistan.
- In the 1990s, the UN played a big role in ending civil wars in Cambodia, El Salvador, Guatemala and Mozambique, restoring the democratically-elected government in Haiti, and resolving or containing conflict in other countries.
- There are some situations where the UN has been unable to help and has withdrawn its peacekeeping troops.

Disarmament

Stopping the spread of arms and eventually getting rid of weapons of mass destruction are also goals of the UN. The UN has hosted many disarmament negotiations. International agreements have been made between countries such as the

So... which one is it?

Nuclear Non-Proliferation Treaty (1968) and the Comprehensive Nuclear-Test-Ban Treaty (1996) that limit where nuclear weapons can be tested

In 1997, over 100 nations signed the **Ottawa Convention** banning landmines. The UN encourages all nations to keep to this and other treaties that ban destructive weapons of war. An international conference in 2001 focused on the trade in small arms such as firearms.

Peacemaking

UN peacemaking helps those who disagree or are starting war with each other to reach agreements through diplomatic means. The Security Council tries to maintain peace and security and recommends ways to avoid conflict or restore and secure peace.

The role of the Secretary-General in peacemaking

The Secretary-General plays an important role in peacemaking. He or she may bring to the attention of the Security Council any matter that appears to threaten international peace and security. The Secretary-General negotiates behind the scenes, either personally or through ambassadors. He or she may initiate fact-finding missions or set up UN offices to help build trust between parties in conflict.

Peace-building

The UN works with its agencies, governments and NGOs, to support good governance, civil law and order. The UN also helps to set up elections and human rights in countries struggling to deal with the end of conflict. These countries need help to rebuild administrative, health, educational and other services. For example, the UN supervised the 1989 elections in Namibia and helped with the mine-clearance programmes in Mozambique.

Peacekeeping

The Security Council sets up UN **peacekeeping operations** to try to maintain peace and international security. Most operations involve **military duties**, policing a ceasefire or making a **buffer zone** (a safe protected area for people) while governments work out long-term solutions. Others may need local police to help organise elections or monitor human rights.

FACTS ABOUT THE UNITED NATIONS

- The UN created the Universal Declaration of Human Rights (1948), as well as over 80 human rights treaties which help protect rights.

- The UN and its agencies, including the World Bank and the UN Development Programme, are helping development in poor countries.

- UN environmental conventions helped to reduce acid rain in Europe and America, cut sea pollution and helped to reduce the production of gases destroying the Earth's ozone layer.

- UN peacekeeping is important for peace. Currently, some 37 400 UN military and civilian personnel, provided by 89 countries, are engaged in operations around the world.

- UN agencies help and protect more than 25 million refugees and displaced persons throughout the world.

- The World Food Programme provides about one-third of the world's food aid each year.

- Smallpox was eradicated from the world through a global campaign coordinated by the World Health Organisation (WHO). Another campaign has got rid of polio from the Americas, and aims at destroying it globally by 2005.

- The UN raises more than $1 billion a year for emergency assistance to victims of war and natural disasters.

- A joint UNICEF-WHO programme has immunised 80% of the world's children against six killer diseases, saving over two million children's lives a year.

- The UN has its own flag, post office and stamps.

- Six official languages are used: Arabic, Chinese, English, French, Russian and Spanish.

Some operations, like one in the former Yugoslav Republic of Macedonia, have been set up to help prevent the outbreak of war. Peacekeeping operations may last for a few months or continue for many years. For example, the ceasefire line between India and Pakistan in the State of Jammu and Kashmir, was established in 1949 and tensions have still not been resolved. Yet, the UN was able to complete its 1994 mission in the Aouzou Strip between Libya and Chad in a little over a month.

❓ Questions

1 What are the main roles of the United Nations?

2 Do you think the United Nations has affected your life in any way?

3 Does the UN have a lot of power? What reasons can you give for your answer?

4 Who are the permanent members of the Security Council? Why do you think these countries were given permanent membership? Do you think this is a fair system? Try to give some reasons for your answers.

5 What stops important decisions being made quickly within the UN? How could the UN improve this?

6 Does peacekeeping work? What can we do to help a country that is recovering from war?

9 The world today: Global citizenship

Global interdependence

We live in a **global society**. In other words, we live in a world where countries and people are **interdependent** (dependent upon each other). With improved technology and communication we can speak to someone on the other side of the world at the touch of a button. We learn languages so that we can communicate with people from other countries and

understand their cultures. The world we live in is one of tremendous change and opportunity. However, it is also a place of violence and increasing inequalities. Although more people enjoy a higher standard of living than ever before, there are many people who face life without enough to eat, without freedom from violence and without a home.

In order to make the world a better place, people have created rules and laws. However, at a local, national and international level, people disagree with one another about what is right and what is wrong. This makes finding a universal set of rules for the way in which people should behave an extremely difficult task. Britain is a **diverse society**, with many people from different races, religion and ethnic backgrounds. The world is an even more diverse place. However, there are always similarities between people because we are all human beings; it is sometimes just a matter of finding those similarities and learning to understand the differences between us.

Legally protecting human rights is the key way to ensure that people are treated equally in the UK. Human rights are the rights we all have because we are human beings (see *Chapter 1*). To hold human rights means that we can expect others to act in a certain way so that our human rights are respected. If the protection of human rights is a legal matter then it strengthens our moral responsibility to treat each other with respect. There are civil and political rights which include the right to life, liberty and the right to a fair trial. There are economic, social and cultural rights, including the right to work, the right to leisure and the right to a sufficient standard of education and living. Finally, there are group rights including the right to development, the right to peace and the right to a healthy environment.

How do we identify ourselves?

People identify themselves with what they believe to be important; this is often a set of values or morals. **Morality** is concerned with what is right and wrong. People behave in different ways when confronted with moral choices and their personal set of beliefs or values helps them work out what is 'right'.

We develop our personal sets of beliefs throughout our lives. At the moment, you probably get a lot of your ideas about what is right and what is wrong from your family, friends and school.

To a large extent, our lives are shaped by the decisions we make. When we make decisions, we make moral choices. We take into consideration a number of factors:

- Rules and laws (religious or civil). In Christianity, for example, there are the Ten Commandments.
- Our experience of similar situations – we learn from our own and other people's behaviour and actions.
- The predicted consequences of our actions.
- Our conscience (if we do something we instinctively know is wrong, we often feel guilty) and our love of others.

What makes people different?

There are many things that make us similar to other people but we also form our own identities by noticing the differences between us and others. Some of the ways in which we make a distinction between people are as follows: gender, age, race/ethnicity, skin colour, religion, sexuality, family, language/nationality, wealth and accent/the town or area where someone is from.

Some people argue that we should not differentiate between people or categorise them (label people in a certain way). This is because some people are **prejudiced** against others because of one of the above reasons, ie because someone is white or black, rich or poor. People are sometimes prejudiced or **racist**, which means aggressive towards people because of their race. This is often because they do not understand people's differences and

So this is your new friend... I didn't realise he was... er... so tall!

similarities. Racism is a particularly dangerous force in society. Recently, there have been violent clashes between white, Asian and Afro-Caribbean people in Oldham, Bradford, Burnley and Brixton because of racial differences. Differences can cause arguments and violence, yet they can also benefit people.

What groups people together?

Britain is a diverse society. People have multiple identities (for example, you might be female, young, white and Jewish) and, in order to live peacefully, we try to respect and appreciate each other's differences. There are many **communities** in Britain, where you find people with things in common grouped together. You can also find nationalism in Britain, where people express their **patriotism** (loyalty) about being **British** (or English or Scottish, etc). Being 'British' often implies that you share a **common culture** with the population of Britain. In other words, people feel that they are included in a country's society.

However, not everyone in Britain is patriotic, and some people think that nationalism is quite a dangerous thing. Yet, nationalism has many meanings, not all of them negative. For example, it can just be the belief that a nation should be independent and have its own government. If you are a member of a nationalist party or pressure group, you probably believe that national unity and national identity should take priority over membership of any other group.

Other people see themselves as members of certain communities. These can be geographical (eg your village, your town or your county), political (eg a pressure group), economic (financial), religious or social (eg a drama society). A community is a voluntary group of people who have certain interests or characteristics in common. You or your family are probably involved in a community of some kind, whether it be a neighbourhood-watch group or a local football club. **Families** are also very important for grouping people.

What is the Commonwealth?

As British citizens we are also part of the European Union and the **Commonwealth**. The Commonwealth is a family of nations who help each other's development and share ideas and experiences. It has 54 members found on every continent including India, Australia and Canada, although members are mainly

If it's really a Commonwealth, how come you're so rich and I'm so poor?

in Africa and Asia (its origins lie in the British Empire). Commonwealth countries share the use of a common language, English, and they have many common traditions.

Most Commonwealth leaders are particularly concerned about improving the living standards of their poorest people without damaging the environment. These improvements will take money and technology. To promote world democracy, basic human rights, equality for women, education for all, sustainable development and an end to poverty, the Commonwealth needs its people to see themselves as good 'global citizens'.

Why is it important to think of ourselves as global citizens?

Not everyone sees themselves as just 'British', some people see themselves as European or even as a world citizen. Global issues are part of our lives in a way that they never were for our grandparents. Television, the Internet, international sport and travel all bring the wider world into everyone's daily lives. Society today is enhanced by different cultures, languages, religions, technologies, art, music and literature originally coming from all over the world.

While writing this handbook in the UK, one of the authors used a computer that was made in China, looked at Internet sites from across the world, sat on a chair that was designed in Sweden, listened to a Canadian pop group and ate an Indian take-away! This is a good example of what we call **globalisation**, the increasing interdependence of countries across the world. We are citizens of the world because we share many concerns and interests with people throughout the world. In particular, there are environmental, political, economic and social issues that affect us all. Such issues require us to take responsibility for our actions because of the global consequences. For example, people across the world need to work to reduce global warming by reducing the amount of carbon dioxide emissions.

What is a global citizen?

Oxfam sees the global citizen as someone who:

- is aware of the wider world and has a sense of their own role as a world citizen
- respects and values diversity
- is willing to act to make the world a more fair and sustainable place
- takes responsibility for their actions.

What are the main problems in the world today?

The world today is a complicated and unequal place. We live in the western, more wealthy part of the world where we sometimes forget that a large proportion of the world still lives in absolute poverty. It is not always good to categorise countries or people, but we tend to say that there are '**more economically developed**' nations (like America and the Member States of the European Union) and there are '**less economically developed**' or even '**underdeveloped**' nations (like Ethiopia and Bangladesh). Geographically, the richer countries tend to be found in the north of the world and the poorer in the south.

How do we measure how developed a country is?

Human development is usually measured by life expectancy (the average amount of time that people live), adult literacy (how many adults can write and read), access to education and people's average income, amongst other indicators. In other words, measuring human development involves measuring all aspects of people's well-being, from their health to their economic and political freedom.

Why are some countries so poor?

There are many causes of poverty. Some of the most important causes are listed below:

- **War** – 95% of world wars and conflicts take place in southern countries. The result is millions of refugees, death and huge destruction.

- **Trading inequalities** – Multinational companies (and transnational companies) are known to use cheap labour in poor countries and exploit people in the south by paying low prices for the south's raw materials.

- **Debt and lack of aid** – Most poor countries owe a great amount of money to the northern countries. The richer countries lend money to the developing world at high interest rates. The UN suggests that richer countries should provide at least 0.7% of their gross national product (the total value of a country's goods and services in a year) as aid but most countries (including the UK) pay less than half this amount.

- **Drought and desertification** – Many countries such as Sudan and Ethiopia suffer from a lack of water. No rain and water causes crops to fail. Previously good land becomes desert as a result of climate change, drought and the chopping down of forests. In 1980, Africa lost arable land equivalent to one-third of the area of France.

- **Military spending** – Some governments of poorer countries have been accused of spending money on the military and defence instead of helping to improve the everyday lives of their people. The North/South Report estimates that over 40 000 village pharmacies could be established for the cost of a fighter jet.

- **Population growth** – The countries with the least amount of food have the highest birth rates. By 2025, it is predicted that 86% of the world's population will be in the south.

What can be done to help poor countries?

For a huge number of people, the world is still one of **'exclusion'** – many people are excluded from the benefits of being a world citizen. If we participate more as world citizens, it is possible that we could bring more development to people. There are many pressure groups and non-governmental organisations that work towards and campaign for a more equal world. Oxfam and Drop the Debt (campaigning for the developed world to cancel the Third World's debt) are just two groups that work towards a better world.

'We shall be eternally indebted...'

'Yes, I know – but you should have read the small print!'

One very important way in which we can become better global citizens is by learning about the very important issues that affect all countries.

What are the key global issues that we need to know about?

Environmental issues

There are many major threats to our environment caused by the pollution of the atmosphere in some way. Some are listed below:

- **Acid rain** – Waste gases that are discharged by humans combine with water vapour, sunlight and oxygen to make weak acidic snow or rain. This has had disastrous effects for life in lakes and rivers, trees and wildlife and people in general.

Acid rain was one thing, but acid puddles were another!

- **Pollution of rivers and lakes** – Industrial and agricultural waste which pours into rivers and lakes pollutes water, eg pesticides and fertilisers run off farm land into rivers. Such water will kill any marine life and can result in nitrates in drinking water which can cause cancer and birth defects. The problems of polluted water are most severe in underdeveloped countries. The Mediterranean and the Black Sea are in a critical state. Oil pollution from shipping accidents also creates huge environmental problems.

- **Toxic waste** – More than 440 million metric tons of toxic waste (poisonous waste from industrial production) is produced each year. This is then dumped into rivers, lakes and seas or released into the air.

- **Climate change** – Some gases in our atmosphere let in light (heat) but do not let reflected light escape. This process seals in the energy and hence the climate warms. This is called the greenhouse effect because the glass of a greenhouse has a similar function. Humans are disturbing the balance of these gases by producing vast quantities of some of them. If we do not stop the emissions (release) of greenhouse gases then scientists predict global warming will continue, rising three degrees by 2050 making earth hotter than ever before.
- **Holes in the ozone layer** – The ozone layer forms a protective filter around the earth which absorbs ultraviolet radiation from the sun. Too much radiation affects the environment and human health. Man-made gases known as CFCs (chlorofluorocarbons) are causing holes in the ozone layer. The international community is working together to limit CFC emissions which are caused by aerosols, furniture foams, refrigerator coolants and air conditioning systems.

Sustainable development

Sustainable development is often defined as development that meets the needs of the present and considers the needs of future generations. Development goals might include ending poverty, improving education, making sure there is gender equality, limiting child and maternal mortality (death) and improving the environment.

Sustainable development encourages countries to be more self-sufficient, helping them to develop and not to take on projects that are harmful in the long-term. Although easily said, bringing these concepts to life requires a delicate balance of the planet's social, economic, and ecological systems and a shared vision of the type of future we want for the world. Sustainable development can come about only if the world's peoples continue to cooperate in both rich and poor countries.

Food, water and agriculture

At the moment, the world produces enough food for its people. However, food is not evenly distributed, leaving some 800 million people hungry. These people benefit most if they are helped to grow their own food and to do so efficiently. Water is also essential for life, yet more than one billion people lack access to safe water for drinking, personal hygiene and domestic use. Also, nearly two billion people do not have access to adequate sanitation facilities. Without water and sanitation, people cannot lead healthy, productive lives. Without adequate food, agriculture and water, people's health, their economy and their environment suffers.

Poverty

'Poverty is hunger. Poverty is lack of shelter. Poverty is being sick and not being able to see a doctor. Poverty is not being able to go to school and not knowing how to read. Poverty is not having a job, is fear for the future, living one day at a time. Poverty is losing a child to illness brought about by unclean water. Poverty is powerlessness, lack of representation and freedom.' (World Bank information on poverty, http://www.worldbank.org/poverty/mission/up1.htm). There is a definite need for a world effort to ensure that more people have enough to eat, adequate shelter, access to education and health and protection from violence.

Energy

Energy is extremely important for countries to become more industrially developed. However, as the world uses more coal, oil and gas (fossil fuels), we damage our environment. Nuclear energy does not pollute but has certain risks.

Saving energy was an important issue to Bert...

Renewable energy sources, such as solar or wind power, are safe but do not provide enough energy for the world at the moment. One thing is certain, we have to begin to find alternatives to fossil fuels as supplies are limited. Some people predict that we only have enough coal for the next 200 years and enough oil and gas for another 100 years.

Health

Health issues can obviously have an enormous influence on development. Unfortunately, threats to people's health can come from many different directions: malnutrition, lack of basic health care, environmental pollution, AIDS and other sexually-transmitted infections, tobacco and drug abuse. Too much of the world's population suffers from ailments that could be prevented with the proper treatment and information.

Children

Poverty, child labour, infectious disease, malnutrition and poor access to education stops the development of many youngsters. For example:

- **Education** – There is no doubt that everyone benefits from a skilled and educated population. Significant changes occur when girls are allowed to learn, and all people have equal access to at least a basic education. For development to be sustainable in the long-term, the world's youth (the citizens and leaders of tomorrow) must have the chance to grow in a healthy environment and to acquire the life skills needed to take part in a rapidly changing world.

- **Child labour and exploitation** – An estimated 250 million children are working worldwide, of whom at least 120 million are working full-time. A lot of the children who are working full-time or being exploited in some way can be found in poorer areas such as Africa, East and South Asia in domestic jobs (eg maids and cleaners), in factories and on farms. There is also the horrific problem of child soldiers, where, in war-torn places like Sierra Leone, soldiers boast about having killed male soldiers before they reached their teens.

Population growth

Recent studies have forecast an end to world population growth by 2100.

World areas/countries	Population in 2000 (%)	Estimated population by 2100 (%)
Indonesia, Japan and other Pacific countries	10	9.5
Europe (including Russia and Turkey)	13	7
Africa	13	22
The Americas	14	16.5
South/Central Asia and Middle Asia	27	30
China region	23	15

World population breakdown:
Statistics published in the Guardian, *2 August 2001*

However, poorer countries will continue to suffer population increases leading to more not less poor people. Countries with high population growth rates tend to have lower income growth and poor access to basic services such as water and sanitation.

Gender issues

Making sure that there is equality between men and women in the world is a matter of social justice. Allowing girls to go to school, making sure women have legal and property rights and providing access to health care and nutrition for mothers is essential for the well-being of world society and an end to poverty. Although more and more women are participating more fully in social and economic development, much remains to be done.

Information and communication

Improvements in information and communication technology are shaping global society, politics and the global economy. Knowing about key issues and being able to make the most of new technology in order to improve production and economics are essential. Having access to the Internet is becoming more and more important in the world.

However, so many of the poorer countries lack basic services and facilities and access to the latest technology is often impossible. For example, schools in Tanzania and Ethiopia lack the most basic of school equipment (such as pens). The problem is what happens to the gap between the 'haves' and the 'have-nots' if some countries do not succeed in leaping into the technological age?

International trade and transnational corporations

It is generally assumed that international trade is important for the development of a strong economy. Through international trade, people can buy goods and services that are not produced in their own countries. However, there is evidence that some of the world's poorer countries have been exploited by richer countries and large transnational corporations in the international trading process.

Of course it's fair. You've got 'no money' and I've got 'an Armani'!

Corruption

Corruption can mean fraud, unfairness, lack of democracy and bad leadership. In the last few years, there have been greater concerns about corruption in the world. We know that corruption undermines the development process for poorer countries. In particular, many countries and NGOs who donate money to the developing world are worried about where and to whom the money is going. For example, some countries have corrupt governments that are known to spend aid on military equipment or themselves instead of their impoverished people.

Conflict

By just turning on the television, you see conflict on every channel, especially conflict and wars abroad. From Northern Ireland to Israel, you see disagreement and bloodshed (see *Chapter 10*).

Science

See the case study on pages 105 to 107.

How has the world begun to tackle these problems?

Solutions to the key global issues include:

- **Acid rain** – Fitting catalytic converters to reduce pollution in cars. Adding lime to lakes in order to neutralise acid and bring them back to life.
- **Toxic waste** – Recycling waste and reducing the production of hazardous waste.
- **The greenhouse effect** – European Union countries have agreed to decrease their carbon dioxide emissions and the UN has a worldwide action plan to reduce global warming.
- **Energy** – Most countries are now involved in developing tidal wave power, hydropower, wind power and solar power.
- **Health** – A global alliance for vaccines and immunisation has been set up. International organisations such as UNAIDS also work to educate mothers-to-be and other people about the

realities of AIDs, helping people who are at risk of contracting and spreading the virus to protect themselves and others.

- **Food and nutrition** – In 1993, the International Food Policy Research Institute (IFPRI), in collaboration with partners around the world, launched an initiative called A 2020 Vision for Food, Agriculture, and the Environment. The 2020 Vision initiative aims to encourage groups of people across the world to work together to meet food needs while reducing poverty and protecting the environment.
- **The regulation of transnational corporations and trade** – Transnational companies such as Coca-Cola and cigarette companies now have to abide by certain international codes of conduct that stop them from exploiting poorer countries. There are also many international trading rules and regulations that countries have to abide by; however, these are sometimes difficult to enforce.

Agenda 21

In 1992, the leaders of the world's nations met at the Earth Summit in Rio to set out an ambitious agenda to address environmental, economic, and social challenges facing the international community like those listed above. It was agreed that all countries across the world should actively take steps to address the key global issues. The idea is that people can help globally by acting locally. In the UK, counties, towns and local areas have outlined ways in which residents can become more responsible citizens, at both a local, national and international level. Below are some important Agenda 21 facts and figures from various local Agenda 21 Web sites:

- By simply taking one less short car journey a week, we could reduce pollution which can aggravate asthma in children.
- When you make a cup of tea or coffee, boil just the amount of water you need and in a day we could save enough energy to light virtually every street lamp in the UK.
- Take showers, not baths, and save enough water each week for 1000 cups of tea.

- If all the aluminium cans sold in the UK were recycled, there would be 12 million fewer full dustbins each year.
- Each tonne of paper recycled saves 15 average-sized trees, as well as their surrounding habitat and wildlife.

A Call for Urgent Action: 2002 will be the ten-year anniversary of the Rio Earth Summit on environment and development. However, it seems that governments and people have not done enough to respond to the world's problems. The loss of forests, water pollution, increased poverty, worsening health, social conflicts and violence continues throughout the world. The review of the Earth Summit will probably ask for people across the world to take more action at a local and national level to address some of the key global issues.

❓ Questions

1 Make a list of all the things you think are important in the world.

2 Go through the list of key global issues (pages 96 to 102) and put them in order, starting with the issues you believe are the most important.

3 How do people measure how developed a country is?

4 As global citizens, what do you think you, your friends and your family could do to tackle some of the key global problems in the world today?

))) Activity

Find out about your local Agenda 21 and think about how you and your school could become more actively involved.

Science and space exploration in an increasingly interdependent world

Why is science so important?

Science advances our quality of life. Pure science research is the backbone of the technological development of society and, consequently, of communications and travel technology. Moreover, science has led to the development of quality of life of people on earth in general:

- Advances in science have led to better healthcare technology.
- Earth observation satellites are used to enhance crop yields.
- In the future, the World Wide Web may be used to educate people all over the world.

Scientists have been amongst the first groups to make successful use of international cooperation. Scientists strive for a common goal that does not have national borders. Their cooperation in some cases has helped assist and encourage further political dialogue and integration at times of political conflict.

The cooperative nature of the scientific society highlights the technological interdependence of nations since, by its nature, technologies are invented by institutes whose research groups consist of scientists from many countries. Moreover, scientific projects have often been avenues for enhancing political and economic collaboration. For example, the International Space Station is a project where the principle goal is science but it involves the cooperation of scientists, engineers and politicians in the east and west.

Are all scientific spin-offs good?

Not all scientific spin-offs are beneficial. Some, particularly military ones, lead to greater repression of cultures. Science is always accompanied by someone's judgement and, in the wrong hands, technology can be extremely dangerous. Nuclear weaponry and technology is an area of science that has been particularly controversial. Another problem to note is that science is heavily biased in favour of the developed world and yet those that most need it are in the developing world.

How has space exploration led to greater global interdependence?

Space exploration has both directly and indirectly led to greater global interdependence:

- Directly, scientists have been among the first groups to be truly cooperative across countries and continents.

- Indirectly, recent scientific spin-offs, such as the World Wide Web or satellite communications, have led to a communications boom. This has allowed more communication between people from different countries and cultures thus leading to more knowledge, cultural exchange and interdependence. Those in minority interest groups can now have a voice too.

In the future, there will be a need for laws about the exploration of outer space to be established in more detail. This is to allow peaceful exploration and so that no state or person can dictate space.

I don't care who you are, you can't park there!

CASE STUDY

Summary

1 Science ⟶ Technology ⟶ Development

For example, a British physicist working at a European science centre in Geneva, Switzerland, was working on experiments to help understand how particles worked. In order to share data and results with his partners at other institutions, he invented a system of putting files where many people could access them. This became known as the World Wide Web. This spin-off from science has enabled increased global communication between people from many countries and cultures.

2 Technology drives the modern western economy. High-tech markets form a large and growing percentage of the GDP (gross domestic product) of western countries.

3 Space exploration, in particular, leads to global interdependence by enabling us to:

- appreciate our common home, the earth, with views from space. For example, the first person to visit space, Yuri Gagarin from Russia, said, 'Circling the earth in the orbital spaceship, I marvelled at the beauty of our planet. People of the world! Let us safeguard and enhance this beauty – not destroy it!'

- study our planet making us aware of global problems relating to the environment; global problems whose solutions drive political cooperation. For example, the hole in the ozone layer was first discovered by satellite. Since then, earth observation scientists have been using satellites to discover how and why the hole formed and what can be done to stop the problem. Politicians then cooperated to establish national laws to reduce the emission of CFCs which cause the hole.

10 Conflict and conflict resolution

Throughout history, the world has experienced thousands of wars. Wars generally happen because of massive differences of opinion between large groups of people. There are many differences that separate us from one another and we must learn to understand those differences in order to prevent disagreement and conflict.

What separates people in the world?

The differences between people include:

- **Religious differences** – There are many religions in the world. In Religious Education you may have learnt about Buddhism, Judaism, Islam, Hinduism, Sikhism and Christianity to name but a few. Some of the major world religions disagree with each other on fundamental issues and this can be a serious cause of conflict.

- **Cultural differences** – Culture is usually about traditions, inherited ideas, beliefs and customs. In other words, a group's culture is the range of activities and ideas of its people. Differences in people's cultures have also caused wars and conflicts. Cultural differences are often connected to religious and ethnic differences.

- **Ethnic differences** – Ethnicity is usually about racial characteristics but it can link to the cultural traditions of a group of people as well. A race is a group of people with a common ancestry usually with similar physical characteristics (for example, having black or white skin). Race has been one of the causes of many conflicts.

- **Political differences** – Differences relating to politics, such as how a country should be run or who should lead a country, continue to be very important causes of conflict today.

- **Wealth** – Economic differences are also the cause of much conflict.

What is conflict?

Politics is the art of solving problems and disagreements without using force. When politics breaks down or fails, force is often used to settle an argument. **Conflict** is a fight between opposing forces. It is usually caused by different ideas or interests. There are many different types of conflict. Conflict can be found between a mother and a daughter in the home and between two large nations involving millions of people. In this chapter, we will consider conflict on an international scale.

What causes war?

In History you may have learned about long-term and short-term causes of wars. For example, the assassination of Archduke Franz Ferdinand in Sarajevo in 1914 was the short-term cause of the First World War. However, there were many underlying long-term causes of the War including the arms race between Britain and Germany and the split of Europe into two rival camps (the Triple Alliance and the Triple Entente). Historians often disagree about which causes are the most important when they study conflicts but, generally, we can recognise some of the most common causes of war throughout history. These include:

- **Nationalism** – Fighting to get rid of a foreign ruler or wanting independence from another country.
- **Religion** – For example, a war between Muslims and Christians.
- **Politics** or ideas – For example, a disagreement over how a country should be run.
- **Ethnicity or race** – For example, the Serbs fighting the Croats.
- **Economics, land and resources** – A war to get better resources (possessions, land or wealth) for a country's people.
- **Injustice** – For example, overthrowing a dictator.
- **Revenge** – For example, fighting because a country was defeated in a previous war.
- **A powerful individual or group desiring more power** – For example, a dictator who rules by force.

Key wars and events of the last 100 years

Over the last 100 years, the world has witnessed many terrible wars. Technology has continued to develop at such an incredible rate that a nuclear war today could see the destruction of entire continents and civilisations. Some wars have been civil wars, that is, conflicts between different members of the same country, whilst other wars have been on a much larger international scale. The twentieth century will be particularly remembered for the horrors of the First and the Second World Wars. It will also be remembered for the Cold War (1945-1990). This was so-called because fighting never actually broke out between the Communist former Soviet Union and America directly, but there were many times when people thought they were on the edge of a Third World War – a war that could have been the most destructive yet.

The twenty-first century has seen an increased concern about terrorist and extremist groups. The attack on the twin towers of the World Trade Center in New York and the Pentagon in Washington, USA on 11 September 2001, may well see the beginning of a new type of war between the democratic west and extremist terrorist groups.

I think you'll find the sign reads 'Summer Bed Linen ... now in store'

Peace

Key international organisations and treaties (agreements) that were set up in the twentieth century to promote peace include:

- The United Nations Organisation set up in 1948.
- The North Atlantic Treaty Organisation (NATO) set up in 1949.
- The Organisation for Security and Cooperation in Europe.
- Amnesty International and Human Rights Watch.

However, military pacts have less significance now than they used to. More recently, associations that promote regional, economic and social development, such as the EU, have evolved. Such organisations promote peace among their member countries by encouraging them to become more interconnected with one another.

Wars

Why do wars break out?

Working out who is or is not to blame for outbreaks of war is an extremely difficult task. For example, if a group of countries invade a country that is being run unfairly by a forceful dictator, it might be possible to argue that there can be such a thing as a 'just war'. **Reconciliation**, which means compromise or settlement, is often difficult because the people who have been at war may be extremely resentful about the actions of their opposition and the deaths of loved ones. The need for revenge is an extremely difficult desire to control.

How can war be prevented?

An Agenda for Peace was a report prepared by the UN in 1992. This report was concerned with ways of making the UN more effective at preventing conflict and building peace. It outlined four key areas required to keep the peace in countries on the edge of conflict. These are described on the next page.

- **Preventative diplomacy** – Preventing conflict. This is action to stop arguments arising between countries in the first place. This can involve watching out for signs of discontent by looking at the facts, and helping to build up confidence between countries.
- **Peacemaking** – Making peace is the action to bring hostile countries to agreement.
- **Peacekeeping** – Placing civilians or military people between hostile parties (countries or groups of people) to help control and resolve a conflict. UN peacekeepers wear blue helmets or berets. In 1988, the UN peacekeepers were awarded the Nobel Peace Prize.
- **Peace-building** – Attempting to reconstruct and reconcile (re-establish friendly relations) between people. This is done by establishing projects which link hostile parties together; the hope is to create confidence which is necessary for peace.

When war does break out, how can conflicts be resolved?

The UN Charter (see page 78) sets out the measures that have to be introduced and stuck to should a war erupt. However, in reality, the UN has limited powers. In other words, it is often impossible for UN peacekeeping forces to storm into a country and sort out a dispute – conflicts are always extremely complicated. Some example articles from the UN Charter are below:

- Article 33 – Countries in conflict should settle their differences peacefully with diplomatic help from the UN.
- Article 36 – The International Court of Justice can be asked by a Member State to decide who is right and who is wrong.
- Article 41 – The UN Security Council may ask Member States to stop trading with the country or countries and to cut all forms of communication by sea, air, rail, telephone, etc. Members may also be asked to close embassies in the country or countries concerned.
- Article 42 – If the above fails, the UN may use military force to stop the countries from fighting.

- Article 43 – All Member States have to make an agreed number of armed forces available to the Security Council for use in such situations.

- Article 45 – Member States should keep a certain number of air forces available for use when urgent action is required.

Unfortunately, due to the veto structure of the Security Council, some people think that UN action is often too little, too late. The veto structure requires all the permanent Member States (ie US, Russia, China, UK and France) to obtain complete agreement on how and when to take action before anything is done. In addition, this can mean action is biased towards the interests of the permanent five.

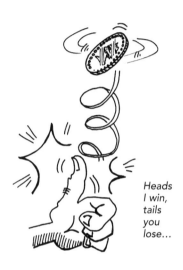

Heads I win, tails you lose...

What are the consequences of war?

After a war, a country or a people is left to cope with death and destruction. Many innocent human beings suffer and the international community is often called upon for aid (donations of money and goods). Listed below are some of the immediate consequences of war. Can you think of any more?

- Damage to buildings and countryside.
- Death.
- Homelessness and refugees.
- Lack of food and supplies.
- Broken families and orphans.
- Resentment, anger and nationwide depression.
- Political, economic and social chaos.

Is peace possible?

It is very important that we continue to learn from the past in order to make the future a more peaceful place. You are what is known as 'the next generation', for you are the next generation of workers, inventors, parents and leaders. Soon it will be your turn to shape the future. History has shown that peace is possible if people really want it. However, peace requires compromise and patience and these skills have to be developed.

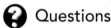 Questions

1 What do you think are the most important causes of war? Explain why.

2 Why do you think that it is so difficult to keep the peace in the world today?

3 Research and write definitions for the following key words: persecution, reconciliation, discrimination, prejudice, forgiveness, racism, xenophobia, toleration.

4 Make a list of the ways in which you think war can be prevented. What organisations/people/countries should be responsible for stopping wars from breaking out and keeping the peace?

Activities

1 Carry out a research project on a conflict going on in the world today. You might want to look at the wars in the Balkans, the Middle East or in Northern Ireland. Within your study try to answer the following questions: What has caused this conflict? Who are the opposing sides? What are the key issues? Look at the way in which the media covers this conflict. Is it showing the whole story? Which organisations are trying to help bring about peace? Is peace possible?

2 Try to compile a timeline of wars in the twentieth century; there was a conflict somewhere in the world nearly every day.

Useful Web sites

As some of the Web sites apply to more than one topic area, you may find them repeated under different headings. All addresses are correct at the time of going to print.

Political and community participation
- British Youth Council – http://www.byc.org.uk/
- BritKid – A site about race, racism and life – http://www.britkid.org/
- CSV (Community Service Volunteers) – This charity aims to give everyone the chance to play an active part in their community. The site has an Education for Citizenship section – http://www.csv.org.uk/
- Children's Express – News and comments by young people – http://www.childrens-express.org/
- Global Dimension – http://www.globaldimension.org.uk/
- Hansard Society – Information on developing mock elections – http://www.hansard-society.org.uk/
- The National Youth Agency – Has a section on supporting young people's community action – http://www.nya.org.uk/
- School Councils UK – Offers advice on dynamic Citizenship Education – http://www.schoolcouncils.org.uk/
- UK Youth Parliament – http://www.ukyp.org.uk/
- YourTurn.net – A site for teenagers on how you can get involved, for example, in politics, campaigning, volunteering, etc. It also explains the key systems in the UK and how they work – http://www.yourturn.net/

Citizenship Education sites
- Advancement Foundation for Citizenship – Offers Citizenship Awards to schools – http://www.livjm.ac.uk/citizen/
- Association for Citizenship Teaching (ACT) – http://www.teachingcitizenship.org.uk/
- Citizenship Foundation – http://www.citfou.org.uk/
- DfES Citizenship – http://www.dfes.gov.uk/citizenship/
- Development Education Association – http://www.dea.org.uk/
- Citizenship Education: the global dimension – http://www.citizenship-global.org.uk/
- Institute for Citizenship – http://www.citizen.org.uk/

Human rights
- Amnesty International – http://www.amnesty.org.uk/
- Anti-Slavery International – http://www.antislavery.org/

- Commission for Racial Equality – http://www.cre.gov.uk/
- Convention on the Rights of the Child – http://www.unicef.org/crc/
- Human Rights Unit – http://www.humanrights.gov.uk/
- Global Gang – News and games from around the world – http://www.globalgang.org.uk/

The media
- Campaign for Press and Broadcasting Freedom – http://www.cpbf.org.uk/
- Daily Record – http://www.dailyrecord.co.uk/
- Guardian Unlimited – http://www.guardian.co.uk/
- Independent Online – http://www.independent.co.uk/
- Sun Online – http://www.thesun.co.uk/
- Telegraph – http://www.telegraph.co.uk/
- The Times – http://www.thetimes.co.uk/

Television
- BBC Online – http://www.bbc.co.uk/
- Channel 4.com – http://www.channel4.com/

How government works
- BBC political news – http://www.bbc.co.uk/politics/
- European Parliament – http://www.europarl.eu.int/
- Explore Parliament – Education Unit Home Page – http://www.explore.parliament.uk/
- Information on the National Assembly for Wales – http://www.wales.gov.uk/youngvoice/
- Information on the Scottish Parliament – http://www.scottish.parliament.uk/
- Institute for Citizenship – http://www.citizen.org.uk/
- 10 Downing Street – http://www.pm.gov.uk/ or http://www.number-10.gov.uk/
- UK Online.gov.uk – Web site for all UK government organisations – http://www.open.gov.uk/
- UK Parliament, House of Commons and House of Lords – http://www.parliament.uk/

Political participation
- Charter 88 – A group that campaigns for modern and fair democracy – http://www.charter88.org.uk/
- Europa – The European Union Online – http://www.europa.eu.int/
- House of Commons – To find out the name of your local MP – http://www.locata.co.uk/commons/
- Inland Revenue – Information on tax and national insurance – http://www.inlandrevenue.gov.uk/

- Learn.co.uk – Mock elections and online debates – http://www.learn.co.uk/yvote/
- Local Government Association – http://www.lga.gov.uk/
- Make Votes Count – Information on proportional representation – http://www.makevotescount.org.uk/
- National Statistics – Provides neighbourhood statistics – http://www.statistics.gov.uk/
- The Department of Transport, Local Government and the Regions (DTLR) – http://www.local-regions.detr.gov.uk/
- Up My Street – Provides information on different neighbourhoods – http://www.upyourstreet.co.uk/

The United Nations
- United Nations – The main UN Web site – http://www.un.org/
- United Nations Cyberschoolbus – Information and ideas about global trends – http://www.un.org/pubs/cyberschoolbus/index.html
- United Nations Development Programme – http://www.undp.org/
- UNICEF – Has maps, definitions and summaries of the State of the World's Children report – http://www.unicef.org/
- United Nations High Commission on Refugees – Summarises current issues and provides information on refugees – http://www.unhcr.ch/
- UN Environment Programme – http://www.unep.org/
- United Nations Association UK – http://www.una-uk.org/

Global citizenship
- Commission for Racial Equality – http://www.cre.gov.uk/
- Commonwealth Institute – http://www.commonwealth.org.uk/education/
- Friends of the Earth – http://www.foe.co.uk/
- Greenpeace – http://www.greenpeace.org/
- National Statistics – Includes national and regional statistics for the UK – http://www.statistics.gov.uk/
- Oxfam – http://www.oxfam.org.uk/coolplanet/
- UN Educational, Scientific and Cultural Organisation – http://www.unesco.org/

Conflict and conflict resolution
- Christian Aid – http://www.christian-aid.org.uk/
- European Parliament – http://www.europa.eu.int/
- The Refugee Council – http://www.refugeecouncil.org.uk/
- United Nations – http://www.un.org/
- United Nations Association – http://www.una-uk.org/
- United Nations High Commission for Refugees – http://www.unhcr.ch/

Glossary

Absolute poverty	When income levels are inadequate to enjoy a minimum standard of living.
Apartheid	The separation and unequal treatment of people because of their race or colour.
Bank of England	The central bank of the UK.
Bicameral	A parliament that is made up of two houses, like in the UK: the House of Commons and the House of Lords.
Biased	A one-sided view.
Bill	A written document presented to Members of Parliament for a vote.
Bill of Rights	A set of rules guaranteeing people human rights and what we call civil liberties. Examples include the freedom of movement, freedom from arbitrary (unprovoked or senseless) arrest and freedom of speech.
Cabinet	This is the group of the most senior members of the Government. Members are chosen by the Prime Minister.
Ceasefire	Where both sides agree not to attack each other anymore.
Censorship	The control of what people say, hear, write or read by a government. Censorship particularly affects the media.
Charter	A set of guidelines or rules that explain the aims of an organisation and the rights and duties of its members.
Citizenship	We need to gain the knowledge, skills and understanding necessary to become informed, active and responsible national and global citizens. Global citizenship, like national citizenship, is about being aware of international political and economic systems, understanding your place in them and knowing your rights. It is about playing your part in helping global problems such as reducing poverty, disease and helping conserve the environment.
Civil war	Conflict between different groups within the same country.
Cold War	The Cold War (1945-1990) was so-called because fighting never broke out between the former Soviet Union and America, but there were many times when people thought they were on the edge of a Third World War.
Common Market	A group of countries who joined together so that goods, services, labour and capital could circulate freely.

Commonwealth	The Commonwealth is a family of nations who help each other's development and share ideas and experience. It has 54 members found on every continent including India, Australia and Canada, although mainly in Africa and Asia.
Communities	A community is a voluntary group of people who have certain interests or characteristics in common.
Conflict	A fight between opposing forces.
Conflict resolution	We need to understand how conflicts are a barrier to development and to find a way to end the conflicts and promote peace.
Consensus	Agreement.
Constituency	The UK is divided into geographical areas known as constituencies. You register to vote in your constituency, as this is where you live.
Constitution	A set of traditions and laws according to which a state or organisation is governed.
Continent	The geographical area of Europe.
County councils	In charge of large budget services such as the police, fire, main roads and social services.
Cultural	Culture is usually about traditions, inherited ideas, beliefs and customs. In other words, a group's culture is the range of activities and ideas of its people.
Debt	Most poor countries owe a great amount of money to the richer northern countries. The richer countries lend money to the developing world at high interest rates.
Democracy	Means 'people power'. The word democracy comes from the Greek word *demokratia* which means *demos* (people) and *kratos* (rule).
Demography	Study of the population.
Devolution	The transfer of certain powers from central government to smaller regional governments within a country or to smaller nations.
Direct democracy	Everyone votes on new laws. For example, there would be a referendum on every decision or new law.
Disarmament	The process of getting rid of arms.
Diversity	We need to understand and respect differences and be able to remember the similarities and the fact that we are all human beings.

Economic	Financial, related to money.
Economic growth	An increase in a country's output of goods and services.
Economic sanctions	Where trade is stopped with the country that is not being peaceful.
Economy	The economy is the management of money, resources, spending and saving. The economy is concerned with the production, distribution (the supply) and consumption (the use) of goods and services.
Electoral register	A list of all those people who have registered their right to vote in a particular **constituency**.
Electorate	The voters.
Emigration	The movement of people from a country.
Employee	People who make their living by working for someone else or a company are called employees because they are in employment.
Employer	Someone or a group of people who employs others.
Ethnicity	Ethnicity is often about racial characteristics but it can link to the cultural traditions of a group of people. A race is a group of people with a common ancestry usually with similar physical characteristics (eg having black or white skin).
Euro	The single European currency.
Exchange rate	The price of one currency in terms of another currency or the price at which any good is being traded for another good.
Exports	Goods, services and capital sold abroad.
First-past-the-post system	A winner-takes-all electoral system.
Free trade	International trade free from any restrictions such as tariffs.
Freedom of the press	The right to publish facts, ideas and opinions without interference from the government or from private groups.
General election	When the people (electors) vote for the candidate from the political party of their choice to be the Member of Parliament (MP) for their **constituency**.
Globalisation	This word is used to mean many things but a common usage of it is about the increasing **interdependence** of countries across the world.

Human rights	The idea that we are entitled to the same rights because we are human.
Humanitarian	Concerned with the interests of mankind.
Immigration	The movement of people into a country.
Imports	Goods, services and capital assets purchased from overseas countries.
Inalienable	Cannot be taken away or removed (eg as in rights).
Income tax	Tax levied by a government on wages, rent, interest and dividends.
Indirect democracy	Representative government where we vote for someone (an MP) to represent us when decisions are being made.
Industrial action	When workers protest about their terms and conditions.
Industrial relations	The relations between employers and employees.
Inflation	The continual increase in prices. The value or buying power of money refers to the amount of goods or services one pound can buy. Inflation means the value of money falls because prices keep rising.
Insurance	A way of providing for financial consequences of theft or fire, for example, by paying a regular sum.
Interdependent	Mutually dependent on each other.
Interest group	A group who mainly defend the interests of a particular group of people.
International trade	The exchange of goods and services between countries.
Interned	To be locked up.
Liberal democracy	A democracy where there are some constraints on a government or the state's power such as a **constitution**, a **bill of rights**, the rule of law.
Local government	The government of an area smaller than a country such as a county or town. Local government has responsibility for the welfare of its citizens and provides certain services such as education. The main functions of local government usually include road maintenance, regulation of building standards, public health, rubbish collection and looking after public facilities such as public parks.
Manifesto	A list of a political party's beliefs and intentions should it get in to power. Issues such as the economy, tax, education, health and the European Union are addressed in manifestos.

Media	Organisations or agencies that provide the public with news information, eg radio, television, newspapers, magazines and the Internet.
Mediate	When someone talks to those in dispute and tries to reduce the threat to peace via compromise.
Monarch	The Queen or King.
Morality	Concern with what is right and wrong. People behave in different ways when confronted with moral choices and their personal set of beliefs or values helps them work out what is 'right'.
Multinational corporation	A company which operates in more than one country.
Multi-party system	When there are more than two parties competing for power.
Nation	A group of people with similar roots and interests that identify themselves as a nation.
Nationalism	Where people express their patriotism (loyalty) about being from a certain country or state.
Natural resources	Non man-made resources.
Natural rights	Rights belonging to a person by nature and because they are human, not because of citizenship in a particular country or membership of a religious or ethnic group.
Opinion polls	Records of what people think on a given issue, often found in newspapers.
Overtime	Hours of work undertaken above the standard working hours.
Paramilitary	Those groups that have a military structure, aiming to use force against another power.
Parliament	In the UK, this consists of the Queen, the House of Lords and the House of Commons. All three combine to carry out the work of Parliament, although when people talk about Parliament they really mean the House of Commons.
Peace-building	Reconstructing and reconciling between people. This is done by establishing projects to link hostile parties together, to create confidence which is necessary for peace.

Peacekeeping	This involves placing civilians or military people between hostile parties (countries or groups of people) to help control and resolve a conflict. UN peacekeepers wear blue helmets or berets.
Policies	When an idea is to be carried out. Policies are made by ministers and civil servants.
Political parties	For example, the Labour, Liberal Democrat and Conservative Parties in Britain.
Politics	The art of solving problems and disagreements without using force.
Prejudice	When we treat people differently because of their race, religion, wealth, etc.
Pressure groups	Any group which comes together to present a particular cause, often called 'interest groups'. A pressure group is an organised group (such as Amnesty International or Greenpeace) that aims to influence government, although they do not wish to govern.
Prime Minister	The leader of the political party with the majority in the UK.
Private sector	The part of the economy controlled by individuals and companies.
Privatisation	Sale of government-owned shares in private sector companies.
Proportional representation	When parliamentary seats are allocated in proportion to the amount of votes a party gets.
Public corporations	State-owned industries.
Public sector	The part of the economy under state control. It is made up of organisations that are either the responsibility of central or local government. For example, the Government is responsible for the National Health Service (NHS), the emergency services, the armed forces and state education.
Racism	Aggression towards people because of their race.
Reconciliation	Compromise or settlement.
Refugee	One who leaves a country or home for safety, food or shelter.
Rule of Law	Where law itself rules and no one person or government is above the law.
Self-employment	Working for oneself.

Shareholders	People and institutions who are joint owners of companies.
Social security payments	Benefits paid to low income groups, the unemployed, disabled and pensioners.
Social justice	Understanding the importance of social justice as an element in both sustainable development and the improved welfare of all people.
Society	Society is taken to mean 'the people' or the group of people who live together in any place or time such as British society or twenty-first-century society.
Standard of living	Refers to the amount of goods and services consumed by households in one year.
Stock Exchange	A market for the sale and purchase of second-hand shares and securities.
Sustainable development	This is often defined as development that meets the needs of the present and considers the needs of future generations. It encourages countries to be more self-sufficient, helping them to develop.
Tariffs	Taxes generally on goods imported into a country.
The state	We say that the state can be a country's people, a country's territory or a country's government. A government is elected to run the state. This frequently involves looking after properties and institutions that affect the daily lives of people who live in the country, such as hospitals, railways and social services.
Trade union	An organisation of workers representing their interests and seeking improvements for its members.
Treasury	The Treasury is the department responsible for making and putting into effect the Government's financial and economic policies.
Treaty	An agreement or contract.
Unemployed	If people lose their jobs and are unable to find paid work, they are known as unemployed.
Work permit	A document that allows you to work in certain countries.